What Regency Women Did For Us

What Regency Women Did For Us

Rachel Knowles

PEN & SWORD
HISTORY

First published in Great Britain in 2017 by
PEN & SWORD HISTORY
An imprint of
Pen & Sword Books Ltd
47 Church Street
Barnsley, South Yorkshire
S70 2AS

ISBN 978 1 47388 224 9

A CIP catalogue record for this book is
available from the British Library

Typeset in Times New Roman by Chic Graphics

Printed and bound in Malta by
Gutenberg Press Ltd

Pen & Sword Books Ltd incorporates the Imprints of Aviation, Atlas,
Family History, Fiction, Maritime, Military, Discovery, Politics, History,
Archaeology, Select, Wharncliffe Local History, Wharncliffe True Crime,
Military Classics, Wharncliffe Transport, Leo Cooper, The Praetorian Press,
Remember When, Seaforth Publishing and Frontline Publishing.

For a complete list of Pen & Sword titles please contact
PEN & SWORD BOOKS LIMITED
47 Church Street, Barnsley, South Yorkshire, S70 2AS, England
E-mail: enquiries@pen-and-sword.co.uk
Website: www.pen-and-sword.co.uk

Contents

Acknowledgements

This book would never have been written without the support of my friends and family. I would like to thank them for their encouragement to keep going and for their patience in seeing less of me then they would have liked whilst I have been writing this book. I especially want to thank my husband, Andrew, who has helped me believe I could succeed, and given me invaluable editing advice, as well as providing the photographs.

I would also like to thank Trevor Adams for kindly sharing his research on the Parminters and Elaine Tovell for help with the French translation of the article on the Parminters' mountain climb. Thanks also go to Timothy Collinson for his help with indexing, and Karyn Burnham and the team at Pen and Sword Books for helping to get this book ready for publication.

Rachel Knowles
December 2016

Introduction

This book tells the stories of twelve remarkable women who lived during the Regency period. Each of them made an impact on the communities in which they lived and left a legacy for future generations – a legacy that's still tangible in the twenty-first century.

When was the Regency?
The Regency was the period of nine years from 1811 to 1820. It was so named because during that time the United Kingdom was ruled by a regent rather than by the king. For many years, George III had been suffering from bouts of an illness that made it seem as though he was going mad. He was probably suffering from the hereditary disorder porphyria. In 1810, his youngest daughter Amelia died and this seems to have triggered the king's final bout of illness from which he never recovered. Parliament judged him unfit to rule and appointed his eldest son, the future George IV, as regent to rule in his stead. When George III died in 1820, George IV became king and the Regency period came to an end.

Although the actual Regency was quite short, the term 'Regency' has come to represent a period of time much wider than the nine years to which it actually relates.

The Regency is seen as a time of glamour and romance, elegance and etiquette. Its tone was set in part by the Prince Regent himself, whose lifestyle was cultured and extravagant, in direct contrast to his father's rather ascetic ways. He held sumptuous entertainments at his Carlton House palace in London and poured money into his building projects, most notably his lavish, fantastical summer home, Brighton Pavilion.

This Regency 'feel' encompasses the years from about 1780 to 1820 – or even 1830. Georgian historians love to argue over the precise dates! The Regency occurred towards the end of the Georgian period.

What was it like to be a woman in the Regency?
For women, the Regency was not always an age of romance. There was

no system of equal opportunities and women had very few rights. Their position was far inferior to that of men.

There were huge variations in the amount of education that women received. Some, with forward-thinking parents, were encouraged to learn, educated alongside their brothers or sent away to school. Most received only a basic education, equipping them to operate in the domestic sphere, with the skills needed to run a household and bring up children. Few received the classical education necessary for studying science. And, of course, universities were exclusively for men.

Although allowed to attend lectures at scientific bodies like the Royal Institution, women were debarred from membership. Despite the fact that the Royal Academy of Arts had two female founding members, Angelica Kauffman and Mary Moser, no other women were admitted to membership until the twentieth century.

Mary Wollstonecraft argued forcefully in favour of the education of women in her *A Vindication of the Rights of Woman* published in 1792. Many of her female contemporaries shared her views though they did not condone her lifestyle, which stepped outside the moral boundaries of the time. Her opinions were in direct conflict with current thinking which largely believed that women's education should be confined to what they needed for their domestic duties.

A Regency woman who acquired too much learning was in danger of being labelled a 'bluestocking'. Twenty years earlier, the bluestockings were a respected group of intellectuals, both men and women, who met for stimulating conversation rather than to play cards. By the Regency period, the term bluestocking, meaning an intellectual woman, was often applied in a derogatory way, suggesting that too much learning was undesirable and unfeminine.

Marriage in the Regency was by no means an equal partnership. When a woman married, everything she owned became the property of her husband. If she worked, everything she earned was legally his. She had no separate legal identity as a married woman.

A woman had little recourse under the law if her husband treated her badly. Usually her only option was to leave. But a woman had to be desperate to follow this course of action as she had to leave everything behind, including her children, because her husband had all the parental rights. Many women chose to stay with philandering or cruel husbands rather than abandon their children. If they had no friend or family to shelter them, a woman could be destitute away from the marital home.

If a woman was rich, she might choose to stay single. By doing so, she avoided handing over control of her money and, indeed, her entire life to a man who might prove to be unkind. She could also avoid the risk of dying in childbirth – a common fate for many Regency women.

However, if she was a gentlewoman without independent means, her options were limited. Remaining unmarried meant she had to rely on her relations to support her, often acting as an unpaid companion in a richer relative's home. Without any such opportunities, she might be forced to become a governess or paid companion, or risk ending up a pauper.

In the lower classes, marriage was still the most usual option for a woman but if she could not, or would not, marry, there were more occupations which she could engage in to support herself, from going on the stage to setting up in trade.

Twelve remarkable Regency women
All but one of the women featured in this book lived through the entire Regency period. The exception is Jane Austen who died in 1817, but as her six novels were published during the Regency and, for many, she epitomises the period, I have not scrupled to include her.

The women I have chosen come from all walks of life, from diverse backgrounds and of varying nationalities. They are not the only women worthy of inclusion. However, each of them made a significant difference to life in Regency Britain, a difference that's still evident in some way today. For some this was at a local level, while others achieved national or even international recognition.

Jane Austen and Maria Edgeworth were both writers from families of the gentry. Both remained single and loved their homes, but Irish Maria hobnobbed with the rich and famous whilst Jane led a quiet life in rural Hampshire. Maria gave us the genre of historical fiction, but Jane has unwittingly given us a whole Janeite industry.

Jane Marcet and Caroline Herschel were scientists and both were very diffident about their work. Jane was an educational writer from a wealthy Swiss family and wrote the first science textbooks for women. She apologised to her readers for daring to teach what she had only just learned herself, yet succeeded so well that she inspired the famous scientist Michael Faraday with her work. Caroline grew up in the German state of Hanover and only became an astronomer to support her brother.

She continually declared that she was nothing more than her brother's tool, but was recognised as an astronomer in her own right, becoming the first woman to be paid for her services to science.

Mary Anning was also a scientist, but from a poor, working class background in Dorset. She was one of the first female palaeontologists and had to sell the fossils she found in order to pay her bills. Sarah Guppy, on the other hand, was from a middle-class industrial family in Birmingham and was both an engineer and an inventor. She made a valuable contribution to the creative mix which produced the design for the Clifton Suspension Bridge in Bristol.

Eleanor Coade and Marie Tussaud were both artists and women of business. Eleanor was from a wealthy Devon family and ran a successful artificial stone manufactory. Many of the pieces it produced still decorate our heritage landscape. Marie came from humble beginnings in France where she learned the skill of wax modelling against the background of the French Revolution. She became one of the most successful female entrepreneurs of her time, establishing a waxworks that still bears her name today.

Sarah Siddons and Harriot Mellon were both actresses, but their lives took very different paths. Sarah was born in Wales and made her name as the greatest tragic actress of her time. By maintaining her own respectability, she helped establish acting as a decent profession for women. From an equally obscure background in Ireland, Harriot attracted the love and respect of Thomas Coutts, one of the richest men in England. Her wise management of his fortune secured the future of Coutts bank and funded one of the most generous Victorian philanthropists, Angela Burdett-Coutts.

Mary Parminter and Elizabeth Fry were both devout non-conformist Christians and both philanthropists, though not on the same scale. Mary Parminter was an explorer and mountaineer who left a unique house, A la Ronde, as well as equipping a small charity to provide accommodation for respectable, single women. Elizabeth Fry was a major celebrity in her time, achieving worldwide recognition for her pioneering work in prisons, which was instrumental in bringing reform to British law.

The challenge of studying science
Brought up in an age when education of women was by no means universal, it is inspirational to see how some of these women gained the

knowledge that they needed to succeed. Today, science is taught in all our schools as a matter of course, making it difficult to grasp that this was a subject from which women were largely excluded at this time. To study science it was necessary to be able to master Latin names, which was much harder for girls as they were rarely taught the classics.

Jane Marcet benefited from learning alongside her brothers, which helped her to study science more seriously as an adult. She also had the benefit of a husband willing to act as her personal tutor, helping her to grapple with the more difficult concepts. She then simplified these ideas to pass them onto others who did not have her educational advantages.

Studying science was more of a challenge for Caroline Herschel and Mary Anning. Caroline had received only a very basic education at home because her mother believed that was all that was necessary for a woman. She had to acquire the mathematics she needed for astronomical calculations at the same time as learning how to use a telescope. Her chief advantage was having her brother's help to answer questions, even if he wasn't the most patient of teachers.

Mary Anning, on the other hand, had no personal tutor. From a poor, working class background, she entered the world of fossils being able to read and write, but little more. Through sheer determination, she taught herself to read French so that she could study the leading papers in palaeontology, and by studying the fossils themselves and dissecting modern-day creatures, she became one of the most knowledgeable authorities in her field.

It is a mark of their achievements that, despite their lack of education, both women were included in the Royal Society's top ten most influential women in science in British history in 2010.

Motivated to marry – or not
It may have been an age of romance, but six of these Regency women never married. However, Jane Austen and Maria Edgeworth both received at least one offer of marriage, which they refused.

Marie Tussaud and Sarah Siddons had unsatisfactory husbands. Sarah's husband was probably unfaithful and wasted much of her money; Marie thought so poorly of hers that she deserted him in France and never looked back.

Elizabeth Fry often left her husband looking after the children whilst she worked as a Quaker minister and carried out her prison ministry. Her husband failed to live up to her expectations, but maybe she put too much strain on their marriage with her zealous commitment to her work.

Jane Marcet was more fortunate. Her husband Alexander was a great encouragement to her and they seemed to have a very happy marriage. Sadly, he died prematurely and she spent more than thirty-five years as a widow.

Sarah Guppy married twice. Although her first marriage started well, the situation deteriorated and when Samuel decided to leave her when their youngest child was only 9, there was nothing she could do. After growing lonely in widowhood, Sarah married again, to a man considerably younger than herself who speedily used up all her money.

Harriot Mellon was the only one who married but had no children. She married very well, twice, though somewhat oddly. Her first husband, Thomas Coutts, was old enough to be her grandfather, but made her rich. Her second husband, the Duke of St Albans, was young enough to be her son, but he made her a duchess.

A Regency woman's place
Eleanor Coade was a woman operating in a man's world. With the inspirational example of her grandmother to follow, she knew that it was possible for a woman to run a successful business. She appreciated the value of the men who worked alongside her in the artificial stone manufactory, like Bacon and Sealy, but she could be forceful when necessary, sacking her manager Pincot when he tried to pass the business off as his own.

Caroline Herschel had been brought up to believe that a woman's role was to serve the men in the family and it was a principle that she never shook off. She thought nothing of her own achievements in astronomy, but wanted all the glory to go to her brother William, whom she served faithfully for fifty years of her life.

Sarah Siddons was acutely aware of her position as a woman on stage and worked hard to maintain her respectability throughout her career. The measure of her success was the royal approval she received and the gradual improvement in the status of female actors. As a married woman, she had no control over her earnings, which legally belonged to her husband, and it was galling to her when he wasted the money she had earned.

INTRODUCTION

Marie Tussaud, on the other hand, had no intention of putting the hard earned profit from her waxworks exhibition into the hands of her husband. Having proved that she did not need his support to run a successful business, she refused to return to her husband in France.

Maria Edgeworth grew up with an enlightened attitude towards the education and position of women. Her father was the single greatest influence in her life and she was always subservient to his opinion, but her three stepmothers were intelligent, educated women. They taught Maria, by word and example, that the best recipe for happiness in marriage for an intelligent man is to have an intelligent wife with whom he can converse. Maria expounded on this theme in her first book, *Letters for Literary Ladies*, in which she advocated the education of women.

Jane Marcet was happily married and was motivated to study science so that she could share her husband's passion for chemistry. She wrote easy-to-read books, primarily for women, which made science accessible to people with less education. As a result, the whole area of science was opened up to women.

Mary Parminter was orphaned as a girl and her cousin Jane became the most influential person in her life. Together they pushed the boundaries of what had been achieved by women before, walking 200 miles through the Alps and climbing Mont Buet. Mary was very wealthy and chose not to marry, but she was aware of how hard it could be for single women in reduced circumstances. She left her unique house, A la Ronde, for the enjoyment of a number of single, female relatives in turn and set up a charity to provide accommodation for respectable single women in need.

Sarah Guppy didn't let her sex deter her from using her creativity in an engineering environment. She was a partner in her husband's business and patented various inventions in her own name. She was at ease talking with the leading engineers of her time, including Isambard Kingdom Brunel, and although her role is played down, she was part of the creative mix that produced the design for the Clifton Suspension Bridge. She felt it was her responsibility to express her opinion if she thought she could offer a solution and, amongst other ideas, proposed a scheme to provide housing for respectable women who had fallen on hard times.

Jane Austen was fully aware of the position of women. She was tempted to marry to establish a home for herself, but came to the conclusion that this price was too high. After her father's death, her mother, sister, and she were dependent upon her brothers' generosity to help keep a roof over their heads.

Harriot Mellon married twice, but never lost control of her life or her money. Although her marriages were unusual, they were both motivated by love, on the man's side at least. By the marriage contracts for each of her marriages, Harriot retained full control of her property, allowing her to be financially independent as if she were still a single woman.

Elizabeth Fry belonged to the Quakers who believed that men and women were equal before God and allowed both sexes to be ministers. Elizabeth became a Quaker minister and worked tirelessly to improve conditions in women's prisons. Despite this, Elizabeth was a woman of her time. She still had qualms about putting herself forward and had a very real fear of dying in childbirth.

Mary Anning had to struggle for acceptance in the world of palaeontology because she was poor and uneducated as well as being female and single. She didn't always get the credit for the fossils she found, but this was equally true for men who sold the fossils they discovered to earn a living. It was the people who had money that generally got the recognition. But Mary broke through into this rich man's world, and her contribution to palaeontology was acknowledged by her obituary in the journal of the Geological Society of London – a society that didn't allow female members.

Despite all the disadvantages of their sex and, in many cases, lack of education, these twelve women made a difference in their time and have left a legacy into the twenty-first century. By telling their stories, I hope to bring a fresh awareness of what Regency women did for us.

Chapter 1

The King's Stone Maker –
Eleanor Coade (1733–1821)

While you may never have heard of Eleanor Coade before now, you may have seen some of her creations without even realising. Britain is peppered with statues and vases and buildings with architectural embellishments that were made by Coade's artificial stone manufactory. Such was the skill with which they were made, these Georgian ornaments have weathered well and you would be forgiven for thinking they had been carved directly out of stone.

Their creator, Eleanor Coade, was a rarity in her time – a successful Georgian businesswoman. Where her male competitors failed, she succeeded in producing a quality of artificial stone that has survived into the twenty-first century.

Early years
Eleanor Coade was born on 3 June 1733 in the cathedral city of Exeter in Devon, the elder daughter of George Coade and his wife, Eleanor Enchmarch. Her younger sister Elizabeth was born two years later. There was also a brother named Samuel who, according to a legal document was alive in 1748, but as he is not mentioned again, he probably died as an infant.

George Coade was a prosperous wool merchant. He lived with his family in Magdalen Street, on the outskirts of the city, and owned several other local properties. His family was originally from Lyme Regis in Dorset where his brothers Robert Fowler and Samuel and sister Margaret are commemorated by a memorial in the Parish Church of St Michael the Archangel.

Eleanor's early years in Exeter would have passed comfortably. She grew up in a well-to-do non-conformist, middle-class family, whose wealth insulated them from the less savoury aspects of Georgian life. Exeter was then still very much a medieval city, surrounded by high walls, with narrow, crowded and muddy streets. Wealth and poverty would have been close companions, as rich merchants almost rubbed shoulders with penniless sailors.

In her home just outside the city walls, Eleanor would have been educated and probably brought up with the expectation of getting married and raising a family of her own. For some reason, this didn't happen. Whether through choice or lack of opportunity, Eleanor never married. Changing economic conditions meant that in the 1750s, Exeter's once thriving wool trade was in decline and with it, the fortunes of the Coades. Bankruptcy in 1759 forced George to move his family, including the 26-year-old Eleanor, to London, and it was here she became established in business in her own right.

Woman of business
By 1766, Eleanor was trading as a linen draper with considerable success. Her stock, insured with Sun Assurance Company, rose in value from £200 to £750 in a single year.

Eleanor seemed to have inherited the entrepreneurial talents of her maternal grandmother, Sarah Enchmarch. Sarah had been a successful textile manufacturer and trader in Tiverton in Devon for more than twenty years after the death of her husband. Perhaps it was her example that spurred Eleanor into starting her own business.

Eleanor was not content with her drapery firm. In 1769 she took the bold step of buying another business – an artificial stone manufactory owned by Daniel Pincot that had been operating for about two years from King's Arms Stairs, beside the River Thames at Lambeth. It was located on part of the site now occupied by the Royal Festival Hall. The firm had been struggling for some time. Eleanor thought she could do better and she was right. Her Coade stone pieces sold for considerably more than Pincot's had done in the two years before she had taken over the business.

It was highly unusual for a woman to purchase a business in the eighteenth century and it is intriguing to consider how Eleanor Coade achieved it. She was in her mid-thirties and, being single, she was certainly not spending her husband's money. Nor was she financed by her father. His bankruptcy in 1759 was followed by a second bankruptcy ten years later, around the time Eleanor was signing the contract to buy from Pincot.

It is likely that she was loaned the money she needed by others in her family. She may have borrowed from her widowed aunt, Sarah Coade, who lived at least part of the year in Lambeth, but the most likely benefactor was her father's younger brother, Samuel. He had already bailed her father out and remained a prosperous merchant. In his will, Samuel specifically forgave Eleanor the debts she owed him, suggesting that he had lent her money to help her set up in business.

In 1784, Samuel gave Eleanor a house in Lyme Regis. Originally called Bunter's Castle, it was renamed Belmont by the Coade family, and Eleanor decorated this house extensively with Coade stone.

Another possible source of capital was a man named John Strange, who was listed as Eleanor's partner in the first known insurance policy for the Coade stone manufactory in 1771. Who Strange was remains a mystery as there is no mention of him being involved in the running of the business. His surname suggests that perhaps it was a pseudonym for someone who did not want to be identified.

Those lending Eleanor the money she needed must have had confidence in her business acumen. Presumably they believed her entrepreneurial abilities were more like her grandmother's than her father's. Conscious that her father had been made bankrupt twice, Eleanor must have been very aware of the risks of running a business and ensured that she kept a very tight rein on costs.

Coade's artificial stone manufactory
Right from the start, Eleanor was in control of the business. All the bills were addressed to her, either as Eleanor Coade or, perhaps surprisingly as she was unmarried, Mrs Coade, a courtesy title traditionally given to Georgian women in business. This has resulted in some people believing that the manufactory was originally run by Eleanor's mother, but the discovery of a few early bills addressed to Eleanor as Miss Coade make it clear that it is the daughter and not her mother who was running the firm from 1769.

Although Daniel Pincot had been operating his artificial stone manufactory with indifferent success, Eleanor decided to keep him on as her manager, perhaps valuing his knowledge of the trade, or his business connections. But the relationship did not last long. In 1770, Pincot published *An Essay on the Origin, Nature and Uses and Properties of Artificial Stone* in which he boasted that he had recently opened a manufactory at Lambeth. There was no mention of the fact that the business was now owned by Eleanor. It must have disturbed Eleanor that Pincot was acting as if the manufactory were still his. Things came to a head the following year when she discovered that her manager was acting independently of her in taking commissions, again behaving as if he were the owner. Eleanor put a notice in the newspapers in September 1771 stating unequivocally that Pincot was not a partner in the business of which she was the true owner, and that all agreements had to be approved by her.

Three days later, she inserted a further notice stating that Pincot was no longer employed at the manufactory. Clearly they had been unable to resolve their differences and Eleanor decided she did not need Pincot's services any longer.

Eleanor Coade did not invent the formula for the artificial stone that now carries her name, but there is no doubt that she tweaked the recipe to get the best results. It was largely made from ball clay – a fine-textured clay found almost exclusively in Dorset and Devon, where Eleanor's family came from. To this was added flint, fine sand, glass and grog – clay that had already been fired and ground to powder. Eleanor called her stone 'Coade's lithodipyra' from the Greek words for stone, twice, and fire – literally, twice-fired, referring to the grog. Sometimes it was called burnt artificial stone.

The addition of glass encouraged vitrification, that is, the transformation of the mixture into a glass-like substance making it impermeable to water. The grog gave the lithodipyra the texture of stone and limited the amount of shrinkage because, once clay has been fired, it doesn't shrink when fired again. The resulting mixture was not very pliable, so it couldn't be moulded directly. It had to be rolled out in sheets like pastry and then pushed into a mould. This meant a mould was needed for every piece of artificial stone that the factory made. However, the advantage was that the moulds could be reused.

The lithodipyra was fired at very high temperatures in kilns that were muffled so as to prevent too much heat reaching the objects inside them. Sometimes a whole design was moulded as one piece; other times, pieces were moulded and fired separately and then assembled. This allowed considerable flexibility in design as the same urn could be decorated in a variety of ways, and statues could adopt a variety of poses. Decorative panels and festoons and the like could be fired separately and then attached to a model with liquefied clay. The firing process, which could go on for up to four days, was a delicate operation. It required great skill to keep the temperature steady in the kilns over such a long period of time.

Not all artificial stone manufacturers were successful in formulating a product that could stand up to the British climate. The firm that made the original Brentford Screen at Syon House for Robert Adam made a mistake with their firing process and the screen crumbled at the first frost. Eleanor complained at the time that this incompetence had affected her business because people thought her firm had made the defective screen, and this failure had undermined confidence in artificial stone. The screen was later replaced using Coade stone.

The excellence of Coade's designs
Having sacked Pincot, Eleanor replaced him as superintendent of the manufactory with the sculptor John Bacon, who had already proved his worth to the firm by the excellence of his designs over the previous few years.

What really helped to set Eleanor's business apart from other manufacturers of artificial stone was the quality of her designs. This was where Eleanor's entrepreneurial flair really excelled – in finding the right people to make her business successful.

Securing Bacon as the firm's chief designer was a definite coup. He was just starting to achieve recognition for his work and would soon be acknowledged as one of the foremost sculptors of his age. He won the favour of George III, sculpted the first two monuments to be erected in St Paul's Cathedral, and also designed for Josiah Wedgwood.

Eleanor probably got to know Bacon through her church connections, as they were both committed Christians and attended non-conformist churches. It may well have been this connection that enabled Eleanor to persuade Bacon to work for her. Bacon continued in Eleanor's employment for nearly thirty years, until his death in 1799.

Eleanor combined Bacon's skill with her excellent understanding of what the market wanted. She also deliberately chose to make her stone an exclusive product. In an advertisement in September 1771 following Pincot's dismissal, she expressed her intention of only doing bespoke work. However, she was happy to sell off her display samples at very reasonable prices.

In addition to the specially commissioned work, the manufactory produced a catalogue of standard patterns. In 1784, the catalogue included 778 items including friezes, statues, vases, monuments and clocks. As making the moulds was expensive, it is likely that all these designs had already been produced at least once.

Bacon was Coade's most successful designer, but Eleanor employed other sculptors and designers who helped the firm retain its reputation for excellence in design. These included John De Vaere, who had been one of Wedgwood's senior modellers, John Charles Felix Rossi, and Joseph Panzetta.

Eleanor herself had some skill as an artist and sculptor. In 1771 she was lodging with John Diemar, a wax modeller and one of the directors of the Society of Artists. It seems probable that Diemar gave Eleanor lessons and encouraged her to exhibit in the Society's exhibitions, which she did almost every year between 1773 and 1780. There is some question as to whether all the work she displayed was actually designed by her, as some of the pieces were later attributed to Bacon in her manufactory's catalogue.

Eleanor kept her eye firmly on fashion. Classical designs were all the rage. Some of the Coade stone manufactory designs were inspired by classical collections such as those of the Vatican and the collections of the Medici. Others were based on the discoveries from the excavations at Herculaneum. Often a design was a copy of an actual item, such as the Borghese Vase and items in the Townley collection.

She also ventured into Gothic design for the gate piers of Horace Walpole's Gothic castle, Strawberry Hill; the Gothic candelabra for the Carlton House conservatory; and the Gothic screen in St George's Chapel, Windsor. One of Eleanor's more unusual commissions was to replicate one of the Elgin marbles in its dilapidated state for Frederick North, later Lord Guildford.

Anything that could be made of stone could be made of Coade's lithodipyra. It looked like stone and if fired correctly, it was very durable and capable of withstanding frost. It compared extremely favourably with traditional materials, as observed in the *European Magazine* in 1802:

Portland stone, marble, and other natural calcareous materials,
are considerably impaired, and, in time, totally defaced by the
chemical properties of the atmosphere; but the high degree of fire
to which this artificial stone is exposed in the kilns, gives it a
durability resembling jasper or porphyry.[1]

Because there was limited shrinkage in the firing process due to the grog, it was possible to accurately gauge the size of the finished piece, which was extremely helpful for designers. It also had one major advantage over stone: it was cheaper. Coade stone was widely used both inside and outside buildings, for statues and memorials, decorating doorways and ornamenting gardens with sundials and fountains. Eleanor had good relationships with all the leading architects of the time, who were attracted to Coade stone because of its versatility, durability and cost, and because she was able to produce multiple copies of their designs.

In 1775, one of Eleanor's competitors by the name of Bridges went out of business. He may have been the supplier of the faulty artificial stone at Syon. Eleanor bought the factory and some of the pieces. It seems she operated from two locations for a few years because, in 1778, she advertised the sale of the manufactory at Knightsbridge, expressing her intention of only operating her business from King's Arms Stairs in the future. Everything was to be sold off extremely cheaply as she wanted to clear the premises.

Coade and Sealy
In the 1780s, Eleanor took her cousin, John Sealy, into partnership and the firm became known as Coade and Sealy. He had already been working in the business for some years and had proved himself an able modeller. It's a small but significant point that in an age when women were generally ranked second to men, her surname preceded his in the business title.

In 1788, Coade and Sealy achieved recognition as the leader in its industry, when the firm was appointed manufacturers of artificial stone to both George III and his son George, Prince of Wales, the future George IV. The fact that father and son appointed the same manufacturer is worthy of note; they disagreed on almost everything else! George III commissioned a Gothic screen and font for St George's Chapel, Windsor, as well as three Coade stone statues for its west front. Henry Holland used

Coade stone at the Marine Pavilion, Brighton, placing smaller than life-size figures over each column of his Neo-classically elegant design. Coade stone was also used at Carlton House, including decorations for the Prince Regent's Gothic conservatory. Unfortunately, George IV had fickle taste and nothing remained in situ: Carlton House was demolished, and the Marine Pavilion was transformed by John Nash into the fairytale palace that Brighton Pavilion is today.

The royal connection continued after Eleanor's death. John Nash used Coade stone to make various statues, vases and architectural decorations for Buckingham Palace including the friezes depicting stories of King Alfred on the garden front which still remain today.

By the late 1790s, Eleanor's keen eye for business had spotted a problem that needed fixing. While her firm's situation on the south bank opposite Charing Cross may seem close to the heart of modern London, it was not an area frequented by the wealthy gentlemen who were her ideal customers. In 1798, she leased a piece of land known as Pedlar's Acre at the south bank end of Westminster Bridge, on the site now occupied by County Hall. Here she built a showroom for people to view finished examples of Coade stone. A row of houses was also built on the land and was known as Coade's Row.

The gallery was in a prominent position, set apart from the manufactory, and was an excellent way to publicise Coade stone to the fashionable set in London who might commission pieces for their large country estates.

The entrance was very impressive. The door was flanked by two columns, each decorated with a statue and other Coade stone decorations. Above the door was a panel showing three full-size figures depicting 'Sculpture and Architecture', 'Time', and 'Fire', with a view of the kiln in the background. The design depicted on the panel was reproduced on the firm's trade cards.

Eleanor produced a booklet that took visitors on a self-guided tour of the showroom, interlacing the information about the Coade stone designs with literary quotations. According to the *European Magazine*, the 'entertaining descriptive catalogues (price one shilling) are delivered to visitors'.[2] The handbook included a long list of places to which Coade had supplied their artificial stone.

In 1801, the gallery took part in the widespread illuminations in London celebrating peace in Europe. This was a great marketing opportunity for Eleanor and she must have been very pleased with the results. The display at her gallery included sculptures of dolphins and a life-size model of a lady standing on a column, and was impressive enough to get a specific mention in *The Times,* who commended the proprietors for their taste and judgement. She achieved another mention with a second round of illuminations the following April, with a display centring on a larger-than-life depiction of the Angel of Peace.

Eleanor must have been shocked and dismayed when, in 1813, her cousin and business partner John Sealy died. She was now 80 years old and had perhaps hoped that he, being some fifteen years her junior, would take the business forward after her death. John was buried in the parish churchyard of St Mary's, Lambeth, and his tomb was, most appropriately, made of Coade stone.

By now, Eleanor was too old to manage the factory herself and she looked about her for someone she could trust with the business. She chose William Croggon, a distant cousin, who managed the manufactory until her death in 1821. She did not, however, make him her partner and the firm's name reverted to Coade.

Marketing expertise
During the Regency, architectural fashions became more austere and the demand for Coade stone pieces, such as relief plaques and friezes, to decorate buildings fell. It was probably this change in fashion that led to the decision to close Coade's gallery. By 1817, the gallery was no longer used to display sculpture and the lease was advertised for sale, with the suggestion that the premises would be suitable for the activities of a philosophical or literary society.

Although demand for artificial stone pieces such as vases and statues continued, the drop in overall sales was a definite cause for alarm. With the closure of her gallery, Eleanor wanted to make sure that people didn't forget her. When she had something new or sensational for the public to see, she made a point of advertising the fact in order to draw them into her manufactory.

Eleanor placed an advert in *The Times* in August 1816 inviting the public to come and see the huge statue of Lieutenant-General Lord Hill. The memorial statue was 17½ft high and had been designed for the top of a column 116ft high in Shrewsbury.

In March 1818, Eleanor advertised the availability of a new design:

the Warwick Vase. The original vase was discovered at Hadrian's Villa in Tivoli in about 1771 and sold to Sir William Hamilton, a great collector of antiquities. The vase passed to his nephew, George Greville, 2nd Earl of Warwick, who gave the vase its name. It was widely admired, but the earl would not allow full-size copies to be made of it. Eleanor must have got permission to copy the vase from the new earl after the second earl's death in 1816. As the original had generated so much interest, it was reasonable to hope that the copy would too.

By this time, Eleanor was describing her business as an ornamental stone and scagliola marble works. Ever conscious of changing fashions, she had decided to supplement the falling income from artificial stone sales by diversifying into the production of scagliola (fake marble), which was now in popular demand for making pillars and floors. It is interesting that Eleanor now chose to refer to her firm's main product as 'ornamental' stone. Clearly she had realised that ornamental stone sounded more attractive than burnt artificial stone!

In 1819, Eleanor again advertised in *The Times*, inviting the public to come and see the 14ft high statue of Britannia, which had been commissioned for the Nelson column at Yarmouth.

Eleanor's death and will

Eleanor Coade was 88 years old when she died on 16 November 1821 at her home in Camberwell Grove, Camberwell.[3] She was not buried in a Coade stone tomb as befitted her long ownership of the artificial stone factory; rather, she was laid to rest alongside her parents and sister in the Bunhill Fields non-conformist cemetery in Islington.

An obituary appeared in the *Gentleman's Magazine*, clearly written by a fan of her products:

At Camberwell, in her 89th year, Mrs Eleanor Coade, sole inventor and proprietor of an art which deserves considerable notice. In 1769, a burnt artificial stone manufactory was erected by Mrs Coade, at King's Arms Stairs, Narrow Wall, Lambeth. This manufactory has been carried on from that time to the present on a very extensive scale, being calculated to answer every purpose of stone carving; having a property, peculiar to itself, of resisting frost, and consequently of retaining that sharpness in which it excels every kind of stone sculpture, and equals even marble itself.

It extends to every kind of architectural ornaments, in which it comes much below the price of stone, and in many cases cheaper than wood.[4]

Being single and a successful businesswoman in late Georgian Britain gave Eleanor an almost unique status. She had enjoyed the freedom and independence of her single state and felt blessed that through her hard work, she had accumulated property that could now do some good for others. This desire to help others was reflected in her will, as was her faith in God. Eleanor made it quite clear in her will that the poor and Christian mission were her priorities. She wrote: 'The Lord's poor and the spread of his Gospel will be allowed by those who know the worth of it to have a powerful demand on the heart of a ransomed sinner.'[5]

She stressed that the way she had chosen to leave her money in no way reflected the affection that she felt for her family, but was determined by the needs and circumstances of particular members of her family which she said gave some of them 'a claim to more special notice'.[5] She also pointed out that none of her family ranked amongst the country's poorest, whom she was determined to serve.

Amongst her numerous bequests were many to clergymen, including not only the Baptist Minister in Lyme Regis, but the Independent Minister and the Church of England vicar as well. She also left bequests to the Baptist Missionary Society and the charity schools at Walworth – £100 to the girls' school but only £50 to the boys' school. Eleanor also wanted to make sure that her maid was well provided for and left her an annuity, together with all her bedroom furniture, kitchen equipment, small tablecloths and silver spoons.

Most of the legatees of Eleanor's will were single women – either spinsters or widows. She knew such women were often completely dependent on the good nature of their male relations. However, she did leave three bequests to married women, specifying that the legacies were for the women alone and were not to become the property of their husbands. She insisted that each woman signed for her own legacy.

Interestingly, one of the executors of her estate was James Stephen. It is hard to be sure but, given Eleanor's non-conformist faith, it seems likely that this was William Wilberforce's brother-in-law, who was the main English lawyer in the campaign for the abolition of the slave trade.

Contrary to William Croggon's hopes and expectations, as manager at the time of her death, Eleanor did not leave the business to him. He was obliged to go through the legal process of establishing the firm's value so that he could purchase it. Croggon continued to manufacture artificial stone for many years, acquiring valuable orders from Nash for the decoration of Buckingham Palace for George IV. Unfortunately, it was probably the failure of George's brother Frederick, Duke of York, to pay his debts that led to Croggon's bankruptcy in 1835.

Although the original firm is no more, you can still commission and buy sculpture in Coade stone today. In 2000, a company bearing Coade's name was established to supply artificial stone sculptures to the public.

Eleanor's legacy
Time has shown the truly durable nature of Coade stone. There are hundreds of examples all over Great Britain and some further afield. It would be impossible to mention all of them, but here are a few examples of the Coade stone work that survives today.

Situated on the seafront in Weymouth, Dorset, is an impressive memorial made of Coade stone. Known locally as the King's Statue, it was erected in 1809, in the fiftieth year of George III's reign, to celebrate his jubilee. It consists of a statue of George III on a pediment, flanked by a lion and a unicorn. Not everyone in the town is aware of who George III was and fewer still have heard of Coade stone, but everyone is familiar with the King's Statue which is a local landmark, where all the buses terminate.

Just along the coast is another fine example of Coade stone – Belmont, Eleanor's house in Lyme Regis, Dorset. Belmont is something of a showcase for Coade stone. The decorations include a mixture of seemingly unique pieces, such as a keystone of a crowned head over the front door and blocks of dolphins, as well as those from the Coade manufactory's standard patterns, like the keystones of girls' heads over the ground floor windows. The house, which was later lived in by the author John Fowles, was recently restored by the Landmark Trust and opened as a holiday home in 2015. Whilst the Gothic font in St George's Chapel, Windsor, was destroyed during Queen Victoria's reign, the Gothic screen still survives. Another piece that has endured is the impressive statue of the *River God* by John Bacon in front of Ham House, in Richmond-upon-Thames, near London. There are several tombs made out of Coade stone that have survived in St Mary's Churchyard, Lambeth, including that of Eleanor's partner John Sealy, and Vice Admiral William Bligh, the naval officer in command of HMS *Bounty* when the crew famously mutinied.

Eleanor's business was not only in the British Isles but also extended all over the world. The entrance to the zoo in Rio de Janeiro is made of Coade stone. The design is essentially the same one that Robert Adam used for the Brentford Screen at Syon and is a good example of where a mould has been reused.

Time has proved the durability of Eleanor Coade's artificial stone, but perhaps the real secret of her success is summed up by an article in the *European Magazine* in 1802 which acknowledged that she had 'formed a school for artists, and brought to considerable perfection a valuable art, which without unwearied perseverance against prejudice and interest had now been extinct'.[6]

Chapter 2

The Accidental Astronomer –
Caroline Herschel (1750–1848)

From the night that William Herschel discovered the planet Uranus, his place in history was secure as one of the greatest astronomers of his time. But much of what he achieved would not have been possible without the devoted assistance of his sister. Caroline Herschel was the other half of a dynamic astronomical duo. It was through Caroline's hard work and perseverance that William's observations were recorded to produce a comprehensive catalogue of nebulae and star clusters. This catalogue went on to form the basis of the *New General Catalogue,* still used by astronomers today.

Caroline Herschel entered the field of astronomy solely to be useful to her beloved brother, but she went on to become a successful astronomer in her own right. She was the first woman to discover a comet and went on to discover seven more. She was also the first woman to be paid for scientific services.

A miserable childhood

Caroline Lucretia Herschel was born in the electorate of Hanover, part of modern Germany, on 16 March 1750, the eighth child and younger surviving daughter of Isaac Herschel and his wife, Anna Ilse Moritzen. Caroline's father was a musician and served as an oboist in a band in the Hanoverian army. At this time, Hanover was connected with Great Britain, as both were ruled by George II.

Caroline's early years were starved of affection. Her mother worked hard to instil in her the traditional Hanoverian belief that women were to stay at home to serve the men of the family. Meanwhile, her father and elder brothers were away for long periods of time on military service.

When news arrived that her father, and brother William, were coming home after months away with the army, Caroline, who was only about 6, was sent to the parade ground on her own to meet them. Somehow she missed them and when she finally returned home, nearly frozen to death, she found the rest of the family already at dinner. No one had missed her. Caroline wrote wistfully in her memoirs: 'There was no one who cared anything about me.'[1]

But she also wrote: 'My dear brother William threw down his knife and fork, and ran to welcome and crouched down to me, which made me forget all my grievances.'[2] This single act of kindness to a small lonely girl stood out in her memory. It helps to explain her slavish devotion to William throughout her entire adult life.

Her father, too, was not entirely lacking in concern for his daughter. 'My father wished to give me something like a polished education'.[3] Her illiterate mother had different ideas about her education, being 'particularly determined that it should be a rough, but at the same time a useful one'.[3] Her ambition was for Caroline to stay with her and be her household drudge. Too much learning might give her daughter a yearning to do something more with her life.

Caroline's education comprised basic lessons at the garrison school and learning how to knit so she could make stockings and ruffles for her family to wear. Her father gave her violin lessons when he could, but her mother objected to what she saw as frivolous and unnecessary, and these lessons had to be fitted in when she wasn't around to complain. Caroline fondly remembered looking up at the stars with her father who was fascinated with astronomy.

In the summer of 1761, when she was 11 years old, Caroline was very ill with typhus fever. She eventually recovered, but it was probably as a result of this that her growth was stunted and she remained all her life a very small woman of only about 4ft 3ins in height.

It was fear for William's health that had persuaded his parents to send him to England a few years earlier in order to escape the gruelling demands of life in the army in wartime. This life had left its mark on Caroline's father, and in 1767, he died after years of ill health resulting from military service.

After the death of her father, Caroline's education, or lack of it, was left to her mother's mercy. She treated her more as a servant than a daughter. Caroline was not allowed to learn French and her brother Dietrich was prevented from having a dancing master for fear that she would learn too! However, she was permitted to study millinery and dressmaking for a few months after her father's death and in so doing, Caroline made a friend who she was to encounter again later in life – the future Mrs Beckedorff.

Caroline later summed up her early years in Hanover as being 'where the first twenty-two years of my life (from my eighth year on) had been sacrificed to the service of my family under the utmost self-privation without the least prospect or hope of future reward'.[4] This sacrifice had drilled into Caroline an intense need to be useful.

A new life in Bath

These grim early years came to an end when William invited his 22-year-old sister to join him in England. Following in his father's footsteps, he had become a musician and, while living in England, had gained a reputation as a musical performer, teacher and composer. William had settled in Bath where he was the organist of the new Octagon Chapel. He had numerous pupils, performed in the Pump Room and organised performances of oratorios. He thought Caroline might be useful to him as a singer. Unsurprisingly, Caroline's mother was not keen on losing her household drudge. William was able to persuade her to part with his sister by offering to pay for someone to take over her duties.

In August 1772, William, Caroline, and their brother Alexander, set off for England. Poor Caroline had to travel in an open post wagon for six days and nights and then endure a stormy crossing to England. Caroline described the boat as 'almost a wreck'[5] by the time they reached port. But her adventures were not over. She travelled in a cart to meet the stagecoach to London and the horse bolted and overturned, spilling luggage and passengers onto the road. Miraculously, Caroline was uninjured.

When Caroline first arrived in Bath, she was homesick and lonely, away from everything that she had grown up with apart from her brothers. Her lack of education and poor grasp of the English language made it hard for her to feel comfortable amidst the fashionable society of Bath. Caroline took over the management of William's household, but that had its own challenges. She was required to go to the market and buy food, but she could speak very little English. The whole experience terrified her.

William wanted to train his sister's voice as quickly as possible so that she could help him. He gave her two or three singing lessons a day as well as teaching her English and arithmetic so that she could keep accounts. He also hired a dancing mistress for her so that she could learn how to move when taking part in oratorios.

William may have cherished some affection for his sister, but his motivation now, as ever, seemed to be entirely selfish. Only the occasional line slipped into Caroline's memoirs suggest she was aware of this, or if she was, that she thought it was anything other than what was right and proper. Caroline was devoted to William's interests and was willing to do anything to please him and make his life easier. William transformed his sister Caroline into a magnificent singer. She sang the lead parts in William's oratorios and looked all set to have a successful musical career. But that career was about to be snatched away from her.

William's telescopes
Although William was earning his living through music, he had developed an all-consuming passion for astronomy. Every available moment was given over to reading about his obsession and learning how to make telescopes. William wanted a bigger, better telescope and, having thoroughly investigated what was available, concluded that he would have to build it himself.

He chose to build a Newtonian reflecting telescope, which was of simple design and relatively easy to make. It was fundamentally a long tube pointing into the sky, with a curved mirror placed at the end nearest the ground. The bigger the mirror, the more light it captured and the deeper into space it could look. Light fell into the tube and reflected off the mirror and back up the tube to a smaller mirror positioned at the point where the image of the sky was in sharp focus, the focal point. This smaller mirror was angled to reflect the light to an eyepiece which magnified the image.

Because the quality of the curved mirror made all the difference to the effectiveness of the telescope, its production was the most time-consuming part of making a telescope. It required hours of careful grinding and polishing and William became obsessed with this task. Sometimes Caroline had to keep him going by popping bits of food into his mouth while he polished, unremittingly, for sixteen hours or more.

William soon began to establish a name for himself in the field of astronomy, making up for his lack of formal scientific education with

31

enthusiasm. In 1781, he discovered the planet Uranus and became famous overnight. He was awarded the Royal Society's Copley Medal and elected a Fellow of the Royal Society.

In May 1782, William was invited to Buckingham House to converse with George III about astronomy. The king was keen to observe the planets through William's telescope, which he set up at the Royal Observatory. Nevil Maskelyne, the Astronomer Royal, soon concluded that William's telescope was better than any of the other telescopes there.

William was appointed astronomer to the king with a salary of £200 a year with duties no more onerous than showing the royal family the night sky through his telescope when asked to do so. However, this meant he needed to live near Windsor and so moved his household to Datchet.

Caroline becomes an astronomer

William automatically assumed that Caroline would give up her singing and retrain to be his assistant, without any consideration of her feelings on the matter. He was right, but it did cost her. Caroline wrote:

> *I had not had time to consider the consequence of giving up the prospect of making myself independent by becoming (with a little more uninterrupted application) a useful member of the musical profession. But besides that my brother William would have been very much at a loss for my assistance, I had not spirit enough to throw myself on the public after losing his protection.*[6]

William was so obsessed with his work that Caroline had to snatch moments in his company in order to develop her understanding. She wanted to be a useful assistant, but her education had been severely curtailed. Over breakfast, she bombarded him with questions and jotted down his answers in a notebook – what she referred to as her Commonplace Book. In this way, she gradually built up the knowledge of algebra and mathematical formulae needed in order to be able to perform the calculations necessary for William's work.

William built Caroline a telescope that she could use to sweep for comets. This had a fairly large aperture and a short focal length and an eyepiece with a large field of vision. With this, she swept the sky, that is, she moved the telescope sideways, slowly, looking for comets and nebulae. After sweeping sideways at one height, she would change the level slightly and go back the other way.

'I found I was to be trained for an assistant-astronomer, and by way of encouragement a telescope adapted for "sweeping" … was given me. I was "to sweep for comets".'[7] In order to observe astronomical features, this work could only be carried out on relatively cloudless nights. Caroline became accustomed to working into the small hours, especially during the clear, cold nights of winter. In these early sweeps, she did not discover any comets, but she did record at least fourteen previously unknown nebulae that she had observed including the companion to the Andromeda nebula.

At the end of 1783, Caroline's sweeping was interrupted because William needed her help. He had finished building his new telescope and wanted her to record his observations as he made them. This telescope was the most powerful he had ever constructed. The tube was over 20ft long and was mounted securely on a wooden frame in the garden. William had to climb up 15ft or more to a gallery in order to reach the eyepiece to make his observations.

With it he swept the sky, strip by strip, searching for nebulae – massive clouds of dust and gas. As William scanned the sky and identified nebulae, he called out his observations to Caroline in a nearby room.

Working for William was demanding. Caroline had to be able to work 'with the quickness of lightning'[8] as she might have to record twelve or more objects within a single minute. Sometimes it was so cold that the ink froze while Caroline was writing down her brother's observations. As she worked, Caroline had a copy of Flamsteed's *Atlas Coelestis* open in front of her to enable her to correctly place William's observations. Based on the work of John Flamsteed, the first Astronomer Royal, it was published posthumously in 1729 and was the most accurate and complete record of the night sky then available.

Without Caroline's help, William would not have been able to achieve what he did. She was responsible for writing down what he saw and recording the precise times of the observations. Afterwards, she would copy up her notes and carry out calculations. She prepared lists of stars which could be used in the sweeps as position indicators.

Over the next twenty years, the brother and sister team systematically scanned the sky and recorded their observations. The results of their research – the *Catalogue of Nebulae and Clusters of Stars* – were published in 1786. The Herschels increased the number of known nebulae from about 100 to around 2,500. This research was later built upon by William's son and then expanded further to become the *New General Catalogue*.

Working with such large telescopes had its problems. Caroline wrote that she could give 'a pretty long list of accidents which were near proving fatal to my brother as well as myself.'[9] Caroline also devoted hours and hours to laboriously copying out William's papers for the Royal Society – no mean task as he wrote seven in the years 1786–87 alone. In April 1786, William and Caroline moved to a new home – Observatory House in Slough.

Caroline the comet finder

William's salary was totally inadequate to finance his research and the construction of the 40ft telescope that he longed to build. Eventually, he received funding for his mega telescope, but in the meantime, he was obliged to make telescopes for other people to supplement his income, including several for the king.

It was while William was in Gottingen in 1786, presenting the observatory with a telescope he had made as a gift from the king, that Caroline had the chance to put the sweeper telescope William had made for her into action.

She recorded her observations in her journal. On 1 August she noted that she had seen 'an object which I believe will prove tomorrow night to be a comet'.[10] It was not until 1 am the following night that she was able to confirm that the object was indeed a comet. She was so excited that she could not rest until she had written to Charles Blagden, the Secretary of the Royal Society, and Alexander Aubert, a respected amateur astronomer, to announce her discovery. She had just become the first woman to discover a comet.

Aubert wrote back: 'You have immortalized your name, and you deserve such a reward from the Being who has ordered all these things to move as we find them, for your assiduity in the business of astronomy, and for the love for so celebrated and deserving a brother.'[11]

The letter that she had sent to Blagden announcing her discovery was printed in *Philosophical Transactions* – the Royal Society's journal – and might be considered the first original paper forming part of a scientific research programme conducted by a woman.

It is not to William's credit that when the letter was printed, he added a note stating that as his sister's observations had been 'made by moonlight, twilight, hazy weather, and very near the horizon, it would not be surprising if a mistake had been made'.[12] It had not. Did he believe his sister incapable of doing anything unless he was there to check it?

Over the next ten years, Caroline was responsible for discovering another seven comets, either jointly or on her own. Six of these comets bear her name. In 1787, Caroline's contribution to astronomy as William's assistant was officially recognised when she was awarded a royal pension of £50 per annum, making her the first woman to be paid for scientific services.

Caroline recorded her delight in her journal: 'In October I received twelve pounds ten, being the first quarterly payment of my salary, and the first money I ever in all my lifetime thought myself to be at liberty to spend to my own liking.'[13]

Her brother's helper

In 1788, an unexpected event took place. In the year he turned 50, William got married. His wife, Mary Baldwin, was the widow of a neighbour named Pitt, and the daughter of a London merchant. She came with a comfortable fortune that allowed William to pursue his scientific career without having to worry about money.

After all those years being William's housekeeper and closest female friend, the marriage must have come as quite a blow to Caroline. The change was most unwelcome and it took Caroline a long time to adjust. She had to move into lodgings and travel to William's house to work. But her devotion to her brother was unswerving and she was still determined to give him any help she could. The marriage produced one child, John, who proved to be a brilliant scholar and pursued an academic career at Cambridge University.

From 1787 to 1798, at her brother's request, Caroline worked on a huge administrative project, listing the errors in Flamsteed's *British Catalogue* and indexing his observations. She presented the results of her labours to the Royal Society who published *A Catalogue of 860 Stars observed by Flamsteed, but not included in the British Catalogue* and *A General Index of Reference to every Observation of every Star in the above-mentioned British Catalogue* in 1798.

William's position as astronomer to the king took Caroline and her brother into exalted circles. In 1801, Caroline was able to rekindle her friendship with a fellow countrywoman whom she had met learning millinery many years before. Mrs Beckedorff had become one of Queen Charlotte's ladies in waiting and was part of the royal household.

Caroline dined with Mrs Beckedorff and while she was there, her friend was visited by Princesses Augusta and Amelia, and the Duke of Cambridge. Conversing with someone from Hanover was a rare comfort and she visited Mrs Beckedorff often, both at Windsor and at Buckingham House. She was noticed by other members of the royal family – the queen herself, and Princesses Elizabeth, Augusta and Mary. Princess Sophia of Gloucester was keen to look through the telescope with the expertise of William and Caroline on hand.

In 1805, Caroline's younger brother Dietrich came to visit and stayed four years. He was unwell and out of funds and came to Caroline to look after him. Caroline philosophically remarked that 'according to the old Hanoverian custom, I was the only one from whom all domestic comforts were expected'.[14]

By the time Dietrich left, Caroline herself was very unwell and suffering greatly with her eyes. It was with relief that she noted in her journal in November 1809 that the doctor had 'pronounced me out of danger from becoming blind'.[15]

In 1816, realising that his health was failing, William urged his son, John, to give up his career and devote himself to astronomy to complete his work. The man who had inspired unquestioning devotion in his sister seemed to have the same effect on his son. John abandoned his academic life at Cambridge University and immersed himself in his father's work. He became President of the Royal Astronomical Society three times, was awarded their Gold Medal twice, the Royal Society's Copley Medal in 1821 and was made a baronet in 1838.

It had been fear for his health that had persuaded William's parents to send him to England rather than stay in the Hanoverian army. The obsessive astronomer had taken insufficient care of himself, and his weak constitution had suffered from too many nights spent outside, observing the night sky, in damp, cold, often freezing conditions. On 25 August 1822, William died.

Life in Hanover
Caroline was devastated by William's death. By the end of October, unable to face life in England without her beloved brother, Caroline

returned to Hanover. Her niece Mrs Knipping later wrote: 'All that she had of love to give was concentrated on her beloved brother. At his death she felt herself alone.'[16] Without William, Caroline felt her life had no purpose. She was already more than 70 years old and thought she was going back to Hanover to die. She was wrong. She lived until she was 97 years old!

Caroline's greatest dread was that she had outlived her usefulness. She wrote to her nephew, John, the year after her return to Hanover, saying that she would have stayed in England to assist him, but she feared that age and infirmity would have diminished her helpfulness and she preferred not to be 'where I should have had to bewail my inability of making myself useful any longer'.[17]

Caroline soon realised that life in Hanover was not what she had expected. She found that she had wilfully moved to a place where no one cared for astronomy and where she struggled to see the stars at all. 'The few, few stars that I can get at out of my window only cause me vexation,' she wrote in 1827, 'for to look for the small ones on the globe my eyes will not serve me any longer.'[18]

She had also left all her friends behind in England, including William's son John and his family. In Hanover, she visited her family and that of Mrs Beckedorff, but found very few kindred spirits. One of Dietrich's daughters, a widow named Mrs Knipping, became her closest friend.

William left Caroline a small legacy in his will. She wrote: 'This unexpected sum has enabled me to furnish myself with many conveniences on my arrival here, of which otherwise I should have perhaps debarred myself.'[19] She enjoyed going to the theatre and buying publications to send to her nephew, declaring that she had to be allowed 'for the sake of supporting the reputation of being a learned lady ... for I am not only looked at for such a one, but even stared at here in Hanover!'[20] When she heard of John's planned trip to the Cape of Good Hope to observe the southern skies, Caroline wished she were young enough to accompany him. John visited his aunt in 1832, before leaving for the Cape, and again in 1838, accompanied by his son.

Caroline continued to be noticed by royalty and Adolphus, Duke of Cambridge, who served as Governor General of Hanover for many years, was always kind to her. Caroline visited the Landgravine of Hesse-Homburg – George III's daughter Elizabeth – who later sent her a fur mantle to wear when she went to the theatre. When William IV died in

1837, Caroline felt the separation between Britain and Hanover grow, as they no longer shared the same monarch. Queen Victoria ruled the United Kingdom, but Ernest, Duke of Cumberland, became King of Hanover, as women were excluded from the line of succession.

Even in her seventies, Caroline's primary aim in life was still to be useful. She undertook one final, monumental work – rearranging the catalogue of her brother's observations so that it would be easier for her nephew to re-examine the nebulae that William had recorded. No small task as the catalogue included some 2,500 nebulae! She presented the results of her work to the Astronomical Society: *The Reduction and Arrangement in the form of a Catalogue, in Zones, of all the Star-clusters and Nebulae observed by Sir W Herschel in his Sweeps*. John was able to assure her that the catalogue was useful and that he hoped to get it ready for publication so that it could be available as a work of reference.

In 1828, Caroline was awarded the Gold Medal of the Astronomical Society for 'her recent reduction, to January, 1800, of the Nebulae discovered by her illustrious brother, which may be considered as the completion of a series of exertions probably unparalleled either in magnitude or importance in the annals of astronomical labour.'[21] In 1831 the Astronomical Society received its Royal Charter from William IV, and in 1835, Caroline was made an honorary member of the Royal Astronomical Society, along with Mary Somerville, the brilliant astronomer, who had been inspired by the Herschels having visited their telescope in 1822.

Caroline was elected an honorary member of the Royal Irish Academy in 1838. Her naturally self-deprecating response was surprise that she should be so honoured when she hadn't even discovered a comet for years. She was also awarded the Gold Medal for Science for services rendered to astronomy by the King of Prussia in 1846.

What was Caroline like?
Author Fanny Burney visited Caroline and her brother in 1787. She described Caroline in her journal: 'She is very little, very gentle, very modest, and very ingenuous; and her manners are those of a person unhackneyed and unawed by the world, yet desirous to meet and return its smiles'.[22]

Caroline was very modest about her own abilities and preferred all the praise to be lavished on her brother William, but even she was ready to admit that her strengths were in endurance, determination and sheer hard work.

Caroline wrote to John in 1826:

You set too great a value on what I have done, and by saying too much is saying too little of my brother, for he did it all. I was a mere tool which he had the trouble of sharpening and to adapt for the purpose he wanted it, for lack of a better. A little praise is very comfortable, and I feel confident of having deserved it for my patience and perseverance, but none for great abilities or knowledge.[23]

She also wrote:

Of Alexander and me can only be said that we were but tools, and did as well as we could; but your father was obliged first to turn us into those tools with which we could work for him; but if too much is said in one place let it pass; I have, perhaps, deserved it in another by perseverance and exertions beyond female strength! Well done![24]

Last years and death

By her early eighties, Caroline's sight was failing, but she was well over 90 before she became too feeble to write letters for herself. As is the peril of living to an old age, many of her friends and family died before her, but she lingered on.

The year before she died, she had her portrait taken. Miss Beckedorff wrote: 'It is extremely like in features, expression, and deportment, her eyes having taken the languid expression more from fatigue occasioned by her sitting for the picture, whilst she is used generally to recline on her sofa, and I see them very frequently sparkle with all their former animation.'[25]

In July 1847, the year before her death, she received a copy of her nephew's work: *Results of Astronomical Observations made at the Cape of Good Hope*. Although she was proud of her nephew's achievements, there is no doubt that she saw it as the completion of her brother's work and it was this that gave her the greatest pleasure.

Caroline Herschel died on 9 January 1848 at the age of 97. At her own request, she was buried with a lock of William's hair and an old almanac that had been used by her father, in the churchyard of Gartengemeinde in Hanover.

Caroline's legacy

Caroline Herschel never sought fame for herself. She wanted all the glory to go to her brother William. Yet theirs was a partnership that produced an amazingly detailed and accurate record of star clusters and nebulae. Without Caroline's hard work, the observations would not have been recorded with such speed and precision. Without Caroline's hard work, the observations would not have been later rearranged into a useful reference tool.

The *Catalogue of Nebulae and Clusters of Stars* (1786), that she helped prepare and later re-catalogued, formed the basis for her nephew's *General Catalogue of Nebulae and Clusters of Stars* (1864). These catalogues formed the basis for Dreyer's *New General Catalogue* (1888) still used by astronomers today. In 2010, the Royal Society listed Caroline as one of the ten most influential female scientists in British history.

When presenting Caroline Herschel with the gold medal of the Royal Astronomical Society, James South, one of its founding members, declared: 'In looking at the joint labours of these extraordinary personages, we scarcely know whether most to admire the intellectual power of the brother, or the unconquerable industry of the sister.'[26]

Chapter 3

The Upright Actress –
Sarah Siddons (1755–1831)

William Shakespeare wrote some wonderful roles for women, but it's unlikely that he ever saw them acted by a female. He'd been dead almost fifty years when, in 1660, women were first permitted to take to the stage. Even then, they had to work hard to overcome the notion that only women of loose character would choose to become an actress.

One of those who helped change the public's perception of females as actors was Sarah Siddons, who became famous for playing tragic characters in late Georgian and Regency Britain.

As Lady Macbeth, she drew from the audience such an intense emotional reaction that ladies were sent into hysterics. She combined her talent with a morally upright life that did much to help acting become a respectable profession for women.

Acting in the blood
Sarah was born on 5 July 1755 in the Welsh town of Brecon, the eldest of the twelve children of Roger Kemble and Sarah Ward. Kemble was an actor who managed a touring theatre company. Life as a strolling player was hard. As far as the acting profession went, they were the lowest of the low. Most travelling actors lived on the edge of the law, as they needed, but usually didn't have, a licence to perform plays. Kemble's troupe was more respectable than most, but still faced the same problem. Kemble often got round this by advertising a concert and including a play in the programme as a 'free extra'.

Although they were constantly on the move, Sarah's parents made sure that she received a basic education by sending her to day schools. She had a natural elocution which her father was keen to develop and a retentive memory which stood her in good stead for her future profession.

Memory was of great importance in Georgian theatre as a company did not perform the same play every night, but had a whole repertoire of plays they could be called on to perform at any time. A playbill dated 12 February 1767 records, perhaps, Sarah's first role, as Ariel in Shakespeare's *The Tempest*, when she was only 11 years old.

A jealous lover

Sarah was just a teenager when a handsome young actor, William Siddons, started courting her. He was not a particularly good actor, but was valued in the troupe because of his excellent memory and his versatility – he could play anything. Sarah's parents were unimpressed. They hoped their bright and attractive daughter might do better for herself than marry a strolling player.

William was impatient to secure Sarah's hand in marriage. Fearing her parents preferred another, more financially secure, suitor, he became deeply jealous and proposed an immediate elopement. But even at this young age, Sarah's moral framework was set. She refused.

This refusal pushed William's jealousy to a new level. He used such violent language towards Sarah's parents that Kemble dismissed him from the company. As a perhaps surprising act of goodwill however, he allowed William to hold a benefit before leaving. A benefit was a special performance where the profits went to a particular actor or actors or to a good cause. Benefit performances were a great source of income to players, often bringing in more money in a single night than weeks of regular pay.

William manipulated this generosity to his own advantage. At his benefit performance, he recited a set of verses that depicted two lovers cruelly separated by the girl's parents, and even suggested that the girl was fickle in switching her affections to the lover's rival. Sarah's mother was absolutely furious and soundly boxed William's ears for such presumption. But William's actions had a completely different effect on Sarah. She declared her undiminished love and promised to marry him when she could persuade her parents to give their permission.

The Kembles made one last attempt to separate the young lovers, sending Sarah away to become a lady's companion in Warwickshire, but when they realised their daughter's affections were fixed, they reluctantly gave their permission. Sarah married William Siddons in Coventry on 25 November 1773.[1]

Mrs Siddons on stage

William and his new wife joined Chamberlain and Crump's company in Cheltenham for the summer season of 1774. By now, Sarah, not yet 20, was expecting her first child. As with all her pregnancies, she worked until just before the birth and was back at work within a month or so.

One evening Sarah performed before an audience that included Lord Bruce and a group of fashionable ladies. Sarah was distraught when she thought she heard them laughing at her acting and went home feeling completely dejected.

However, the next day, William was stopped in the street by Lord Bruce. He asked after Sarah, complimenting her acting and explaining that the ladies had been so emotionally overcome by her performance that they were completely indisposed that morning. William hurried home to let Sarah know that her performance had been well received after all. Later, one of the ladies, Henrietta Boyle, called in person. She became 'the earliest encourager of her genius'[2] and Sarah's staunch supporter and friend for the rest of her life.

Word of Sarah's talent reached David Garrick, London's leading actor and theatre manager. Eventually he was convinced of her ability and offered her an engagement at the prestigious Theatre Royal in Drury Lane.

Sarah Siddons's career on the London stage did not begin well. It was delayed by the birth of her second child, Sally. She finally made her debut performance on 29 December 1775 as Portia in Shakespeare's *The Merchant of Venice*. It was not a role that showcased her talents. She was overcome by nerves and the critics judged her performance as ordinary.

Despite her lack of success, Sarah persisted in order to support her family as she was earning far more than her husband. When the London theatres closed for the summer, she went to Birmingham, where she played alongside respected actor John Henderson. Recognising Sarah's genius he declared 'she was an actress who never had had an equal, nor would ever have a superior'.[3]

But whilst in Birmingham, Sarah received an unexpected piece of bad news: the playwright and politician Richard Brinsley Sheridan had taken over the management of the Drury Lane Theatre and had no need of her services. Sarah was devastated. Her self-confidence plummeted and she was almost completely overcome with disappointment. Somehow, she managed to rally and throw herself once more into her profession. London might not want her, but the provincial theatres loved her. Sarah acted to great acclaim in Manchester, Liverpool and York. Surprisingly, during her time in Manchester, one of her most successful characters was a male role – Shakespeare's Hamlet!

During the winter season of 1778, Sarah was engaged to play at Bath for three nights a week. On alternate nights, the tireless and again pregnant Sarah, played at nearby Bristol. Because the Bath audience preferred comedy, Sarah, with her preference for tragedy, was given the leading role on the quietest night of the week, a Thursday. Fewer people attended the theatre on a Thursday because that was the night of the cotillion balls at the Assembly Rooms.

Sarah Siddons changed all that. Thursdays became the most popular nights at the theatre. The people of Bath discovered a love for high tragedy and for Sarah as its tragic heroine.

Sarah's reputation continued to grow and she developed some of her most memorable parts including three Shakespearian roles: Queen Katherine in *Henry VIII*, Constance in *King John* and Lady Macbeth in *Macbeth*. She gained the patronage of many ladies of fashion including Georgiana Cavendish, Duchess of Devonshire, and Hester Thrale.

Hearing of her success, Sheridan tried to persuade Sarah to return to London. She was not interested at first, preferring the security of her reputation in Bath. But with another baby on the way, she saw the need to increase her income and finally accepted Sheridan's offer.

It was with some trepidation that Sarah stepped out, once more, onto the London stage, fearing a second rejection by the London audience. On 10 October 1782, she played Isabella in Southerne's tragedy, *The Fatal Marriage*, with her 8-year-old son Henry as the child. Her acting was so convincing that during a rehearsal her son thought she was really dying and burst into tears.

Sarah, now in her late twenties, was received with tumultuous applause and the newspapers were overwhelmingly in her favour. In the months that followed, she gained a reputation for eliciting the most extreme reactions from her audience with ladies frequently going into hysterics during her performances. Sarah was crowned the 'Queen of Tragedy'.

'This actress, like a resistless torrent, has borne down all before her. Her merit, which is certainly very extensive in tragic characters, seems to have swallowed up all remembrance of present and past performers.'[4]

Royal patronage

Sarah Siddons made tragedy fashionable, and it was a high compliment to her talent that she attracted the patronage of King George III and Queen Charlotte. Their Majesties much preferred comedy but, hearing of Sarah's reputation, they went to see her perform in January 1783. They were so impressed that they went back repeatedly to see her in all her different roles.

Following this, Sarah was invited to Buckingham House. Respectability was of the utmost importance to the king and queen, so the royal summons indicated that, though she was an actress, they had a very high opinion of her ability and integrity. She was to read to the royal family. It was a nerve-racking experience. Sarah had to wear full court dress and remain standing throughout. Although offered refreshments, she was afraid to accept as she would have had to walk backwards out of the royals' presence and was afraid of slipping. Sarah heard later that the queen was impressed with how confident she had seemed. The queen gave Sarah the role of 'reading preceptress to the Princesses'.[5] This honorary position required Sarah to read to the royal family from time to time.

Queen Charlotte's respect for Sarah deepened further a few years later, in 1788. During one of Sarah's visits, George III handed her a piece of paper which was completely blank, apart from his signature. It appeared the king intended to provide for her financially and that he was inviting her to name her price.

Sarah knew at once that the king was not behaving normally. Such an action was totally out of character. Without a second thought, she handed the paper over to Queen Charlotte. Her fears proved to be well founded. The king became mentally incapacitated over the coming months and although he recovered for a while, this was the illness that eventually led to the appointment of his son as Prince Regent.

Difficult times

In 1784, Sarah went on an acting tour of Ireland. It was not an unmitigated success. She found it difficult to establish a rapport with her audience and was insulted in the press. Worse, she was accused of being mean in her dealings with two actors who were unable to work through ill health. The newspapers relished the opportunity to bring down a renowned actress and the story spread to London.

When Sarah went on stage at the start of the London season, the audience hissed and booed at her with repeated cries of 'Off! Off!' Distraught, Sarah left the stage, but after a while, she was persuaded to face the audience again. This time they were silent. She declared her innocence of the charges brought against her and trusted in the public not to subject her to unmerited insult. Her bravery won the day. In due course, the accusations were proved to be false by the supposedly injured parties writing letters to the newspapers supporting Sarah's innocence.

In early 1785, aged 29, Sarah played her iconic role of Lady Macbeth in London for the first time. As usual, she prepared for the part in solitude. She spent time absorbing her character. She did not *act* Lady Macbeth – she *became* Lady Macbeth.

Having studied the part in depth, Sarah bravely developed a new approach to the sleepwalking scene. Previously, actresses had glided in as if in a floaty, dreamlike state, but having studied how people behaved when sleepwalking, Sarah believed their actions were more forceful, as if they were awake. She also decided to put the candle down after making her entrance, leaving both hands free for acting the rest of the scene.

Sheridan begged her to change her mind about these alterations. Any deviation from customary practice was potentially disastrous. Sarah was resolute, and her innovation was received with enthusiasm. The part of Lady Macbeth now belonged to Mrs Siddons and Mrs Siddons alone.

Sarah was also innovative in her approach to theatrical costume. Most actresses performed in the Georgian fashions of the day, with powdered hair and hooped petticoats, without any consideration of their character's historical context. In contrast, Sarah made an effort to dress appropriately for the parts she was playing.

Every summer, she acted in the provincial theatres or paid lengthy visits to her friends, including Hester Piozzi and the sculptor Anne Seymour Damer of Strawberry Hill. It may have been through her friendship with Anne that Sarah became quite a good sculptor herself.

Sarah's motivation for leaving Bath was the potential for earning more money in London. Her husband, William, had long since abandoned his own acting career and she was single-handedly supporting her family despite constant battles with ill health, pregnancy and grief. Over a period of fifteen years, Sarah had given birth to six children and suffered the grief of losing two of them, one as a baby, and Eliza as a little girl in 1788.

William's chief role was to manage the money. He negotiated the terms of her employment and, as her husband, he legally owned every penny that she earned. Sometimes William lost money on unprofitable speculations, which undermined Sarah's confidence in him.

She also had little confidence in the financial management of her London employer, Sheridan. A brilliant playwright, he was a poor theatre manager, notorious for not paying his bills or his staff, including his actors and actresses. Even when her brother, John Kemble, became stage manager in 1788, Sheridan still retained control of the money. Sarah doubted William's ability to deal with Sheridan, but was not sure she could do any better.

In 1789, owed a considerable amount of back-pay, Sarah's patience with Sheridan ran out and she refused to work. Sheridan mistakenly thought he could do without her and let her go. He was wrong. The audience was crying out for tragedy and by the following autumn, Sheridan was begging her to come back. Somehow he charmed Sarah back to work despite the fact he still owed her money. Sheridan's failure to pay meant Sarah had to keep working in the provinces during the summer. It might bring less fame, but at least she was paid.

In 1791, Sheridan started to rebuild the Drury Lane Theatre and until 1794, when the new theatre opened, the company performed at the Haymarket Theatre.

Family issues

In 1793, her two eldest daughters, Sally aged 18 and Maria aged 14, returned home after a few years at a boarding school in Calais. The girls had inherited their mother's good looks and Sarah enjoyed taking them around with her. At the same time, she was expecting her last child, Cecilia, who was born the following year.

Sarah's relationship with William was strained and there were rumours of his having affairs that may well have been based on truth. But it was not her marriage that caused her the greatest anxiety over the next few years.

Since her days in Bath, Sarah had been close friends with the portrait artist Thomas Lawrence who was, perhaps, a little smitten with the famous actress and often painted her portrait. Lawrence was young, handsome and dangerously charismatic. Before long, the inevitable happened. Lawrence fell in love with Sarah's older daughter and, unsurprisingly, Sally returned his affections. However much Sarah liked Lawrence, he was not in a good position financially. When Lawrence proposed marriage, Sally's parents refused to give their consent.

Before the state of his finances improved, Lawrence changed his mind. As Maria grew up, she outshone her sister in beauty and Lawrence acknowledged he had been mistaken and transferred his affections to her instead. Sally nobly stepped aside. This did not change the way that Sarah felt about Lawrence as a husband for one of her daughters, and so Lawrence and Maria were forced to meet secretly, often late at night. Maria became unwell. She was dying of consumption. As her condition deteriorated, her parents grudgingly sanctioned the engagement and Lawrence was allowed to call.

However, when the fickle Lawrence visited his sick fiancée, it was the serene Sally nursing her petulant younger sister who once again caught his attention. When Lawrence confessed that his affections had returned to Sally, Sarah should have banished him. After all, such wavering affections were hardly a sought-after quality in a husband. For some reason, whether her own soft spot for Lawrence or the fear of scandal, Sarah was far more sympathetic towards Lawrence than he deserved.

But even on her deathbed, Maria was not about to let Lawrence go. If she couldn't have him, then neither could her sister. Maria made Sally promise, in the presence of witnesses, that she would never marry Lawrence. Maria died in Bristol in October 1798. Whether Sally felt bound by her promise or not is hard to tell, but she did not marry Lawrence.

From Drury Lane to Covent Garden

At the end of the 1801-2 season, Sarah Siddons resigned from the Drury Lane Theatre. Why she had continued to act for Sheridan when he failed repeatedly to pay her is a mystery, but finally she had had enough of Sheridan's broken promises.

However, Sarah nearly made her exit from Drury Lane in even more dramatic fashion. One night in April 1802, Sarah's theatrical career, and indeed her life, almost came to an abrupt end. Whilst playing Hermione in *The Winter's Tale*, the edge of her costume was blown over one of the stage lamps and caught fire. Totally oblivious to the danger she was in, Sarah continued acting. Meanwhile, one of the stage hands crawled to her rescue and extinguished the flames. If it hadn't been for this man's quick reactions, Sarah may well have been burnt to death.

That summer, Sarah went on a tour of Ireland to replace the money that Sheridan had failed to pay her. One of the parts she played to acclaim was the role of Hamlet. Her swordplay won particular praise, no doubt as the result of the lessons she had taken from a fencing master named Galindo. Unfortunately, these lessons had other consequences. Sarah allowed Galindo and his wife to become her intimate friends, a choice she would later regret.

Whilst Sarah continued her tour, refilling the family coffers, her daughter Sally became very unwell. Rather than telling his wife and advising her to come home, William urged Sarah to stay in Ireland and earn more money. When Sarah finally got word that Sally was desperately ill, she travelled home as quickly as she could. But it was too late – Sally died before she was able to reach home. Sarah was devastated. She had now lost four daughters and only her youngest, Cecilia, was left.

During this time, Sarah's brother John Kemble became part owner of the Covent Garden Theatre. Sarah was engaged to perform there in the autumn of 1803.

Suffering from the grief of Sally's death, Sarah was emotionally vulnerable, and allowed the Galindos to exercise an undue influence over her. With Sarah's help, the Galindos gained employment at the Covent Garden Theatre. When her brother found out what she had done, he was furious. He considered the Galindos beneath her and in the event, he was proved right. Sarah lent them £1,000 to invest in a theatre in Manchester. In 1809, when the venture failed and Sarah tried to reclaim her money, Mrs Galindo published a pamphlet accusing Sarah of having an affair with her husband and ruining both her marriage and her fortunes. Happily, no one paid much attention to it.

Sarah was engaged by the Covent Garden Theatre until her retirement during the Regency, in 1812. Some years she performed more than others, depending on the state of her health, but she never failed to perform unless she was really unwell.

In the summer of 1804, Sarah and William moved to a cottage in Hampstead in the hope that the country air would ease the symptoms of the rheumatoid arthritis they were both suffering from. When traditional methods failed to bring any improvement in her condition, Sarah tried the rather radical treatment of electricity. Although extremely painful, it made her feel much better and she was able to go back to London and resume her work. Sarah didn't perform many times during the 1804-5 season, however, partly due to her ill health, and partly because tragedy had temporarily gone out of fashion. The boy actor William Betty took the town by storm and everyone flocked to see him.

The treatment was not so effective for Sarah's husband, though, and William decided to settle permanently in Bath, as taking the waters there seemed to bring him some relief. Sarah joined her husband in Bath whenever her work engagements permitted, but this meant that the couple spent long periods of time living in different cities. An early biographer claimed that it was only William's ill health that forced them to live apart. Other biographers have claimed that infidelities on William's part were responsible for some of Sarah's health problems. Whatever the true state of her affections, Sarah still referred to William as 'my honest worthy husband'[6] and affectionately called him Sid. William was taken ill quite suddenly and died on 11 March 1808.

On 20 September 1808, the Covent Garden Theatre was burnt to the ground. All the scenery, the wardrobe, Handel's organ and heaps of unpublished manuscripts were lost forever in the flames, along with all Sarah's costumes and jewellery that she had collected over the previous thirty years. There was also terrible loss of life. More than twenty people died, many of them firemen, killed as they tried to stem the blaze when the colonnade collapsed, burying them in rubble.

Whilst the theatre was being rebuilt, the company played at the Opera House and later at the Haymarket Theatre. The new building opened on 18 September 1809 to a whole new problem. To try to recoup the cost of rebuilding the theatre, John Kemble decided to put the prices up. This led to the 'OP' or 'Old Prices' riots. Performances were disturbed for months by loud demonstrations against the increase in ticket costs. Sarah wisely stayed away.

What was Sarah like?
Sarah was painted numerous times by the foremost artists of the day including Sir Thomas Lawrence and Sir Joshua Reynolds. Reynolds's portrait of Sarah as *The Tragic Muse*, painted during the 1783-4 season, is one of the most famous images of her.

Sarah was above average height for a woman, with a well-rounded figure which gave her a majestic presence on stage. Her face was attractive with fine, strong features which never looked coarse or unfeminine, regardless of the expression that was on her face. It has been described as being 'so thoroughly harmonized when quiescent, and so expressive when impassioned, that most people think her more beautiful than she is.'[7] Her eyes were bright and expressive 'contracting to disdain, or dilating with the emotions of sympathy, or pity, or anguish.'[7]

Her voice was naturally plaintive in tone but she could vary it without notice to become deep or piercing and it was said that her 'wild shriek absolutely harrows up the soul'.[7]

When she was amongst friends and family, Sarah's conversation was relaxed and she was perfectly agreeable, but amongst strangers, she did not shine. She had rather a solemn manner which made some people think her proud. When the author Fanny Burney met her, she was disappointed. Sarah's aloofness was partly a defence mechanism. She was aware that being an actress could leave her open to insult or people taking liberties with her, behaving with more familiarity than their acquaintance merited. On top of this, she had an inability to engage in small talk. She chose to guard her respectability by declining many invitations, devoting herself rather to her career and her family.

Life off the stage
The life of an actress was gruelling. The emotional energy that Sarah poured into her roles left her feeling exhausted. Although so often in the public eye, Sarah longed for rest.

On 29 June 1812, she gave her farewell performance at Covent Garden. It seemed that all London wanted to see her make her final bow. Appropriately, the play was *Macbeth*, and after she had played the famous sleepwalking scene, the audience was so full of applause that the performance could go on no longer and stopped there.

The season after she retired, Sarah delivered public readings from Milton and Shakespeare at the Argyll Rooms on Regent Street. She gave six performances at half a guinea a seat realising an estimated £1,300 in profit. Sarah stood at her reading desk all dressed in white in front of a large red screen with a light behind it. 'As the head moved, a bright circular irradiation seemed to wave around its outline, which gave to a classic mind the impression, that the priestess of Apollo stood.'[8] The intimate atmosphere of these sessions allowed the audience to see every nuance of her facial expressions, some of which had been lost on the huge platform of the London stage. When her memory wavered, she used a pair of spectacles, but these 'were handled and waved so gracefully that you could not have wished her to be without them'.[9]

Author Maria Edgeworth attended one of these readings and wrote:

> *Queen Katherine was a character peculiarly suited to her time of life and to reading. There was nothing that required gesture or vehemence incompatible with the sitting attitude. The composure and dignity, and the sort of suppressed feeling, and touches, not bursts of tenderness, of matronly, not youthful tenderness, were all favourable to the general effect. I quite forgot to applaud – I thought she was what she appeared.*[10]

When the series of readings had finished, Sarah was invited to read at the universities of Oxford and Cambridge, an honour which, like reading for the royal family, was reward in itself.

Although continually urged to return to the stage, Sarah had the sense to refuse. There were a few exceptions for family and royalty. In 1815, her son Harry died of consumption. He was the manager of the Edinburgh theatre and Sarah gave a series of benefit performances in Edinburgh to raise money for his family.

Sarah continued to be patronised by royalty. She read to the royal family at Windsor and the queen gave her a magnificent gold chain, with a cross of many-coloured jewels, in grateful thanks. In 1816, she resumed her role of Lady Macbeth for a few nights at Princess Charlotte's request. In the event, the princess was unwell and missed the performance she had commanded and so she never did see Sarah Siddons play her most famous role.

After her retirement, Sarah was able to indulge her passion for sculpting and she set aside a room for that purpose when she moved to a house in Upper Baker Street in 1817. Her brother, John Kemble, also retired from the stage. He moved to Switzerland for his health and Sarah visited him in 1821. A year later, she published a children's paraphrase of Milton's *Paradise Lost* – her favourite divine poem.

Sarah suffered greatly from erysipelas, a bacterial infection which kept on recurring, producing ugly red patches on her skin, together with other symptoms. This was debilitating in body and mind and it was very disfiguring and particularly distressing to an actress who was always in the public eye. It was a severe attack of erysipelas that led to Sarah's death on 8 June 1831. Sarah was buried on 15 June and the funeral procession was honoured by members of both Covent Garden and Drury Lane theatres. Around 5,000 mourners paid tribute to the greatest actress the city had ever known. A curious incident occurred at her graveside. A heavily veiled lady gave vent to her grief with loud wails and cries as befitted the Queen of Tragedy. No one knew who she was and her identity remains a mystery.

Sarah's legacy
The greatest legacy that Sarah left was in helping to establish acting as a reputable career for a woman. She was a married lady and avoided the slightest hint of impropriety, despite her husband's probable affairs. By keeping her distance from those who might take advantage of her position, she maintained an absolute respectability that gained her the support of the royal family and helped secure a positive reputation for women in her profession. She also helped establish the practice of actors and actresses dressing for their parts, rather than wearing contemporary fashions.

Sarah Siddons was the most famous tragic actress of her time. Had she lived in the film era, her brilliance would have been captured for posterity. As it is, we are left only with the impressions that she made on her contemporaries. It was said of her: 'She must be seen to be known.'[11]

Chapter 4

Entrepreneur Extraordinaire – Marie Tussaud (1761–1850)

Generations of children and their parents have been shocked and intrigued by the Chamber of Horrors at Madame Tussaud's waxworks in London. What most of today's visitors to one of Britain's premier tourist attractions do not appreciate is that viewing wax recreations of the famous and infamous was also a popular Georgian pastime. That the art and showmanship of the waxworks has endured into the modern age is largely down to the entrepreneurial flair, technical skill and dogged single-mindedness of Georgian businesswoman Madame Tussaud herself.

Early years

Much of what we know about the early life of Marie Grosholtz, who later became Madame Tussaud, comes from her own memoirs. Never one to miss an opportunity to entertain and make a profit, these recollections of her early years are colourful and not altogether reliable.

According to her memoirs, Marie was born in Bern, Switzerland, in 1760, the posthumous daughter of Johann Joseph Grosholtz, a German soldier who served in the Seven Years' War, and Anne-Marie Walder, a Swiss clergyman's daughter, who had several sons by a previous marriage.

However, records show that Anna Maria Grosholtz was baptised on 7 December 1761 in a Catholic church in Strasbourg, France – the same church where her mother was baptised eighteen years earlier. As Marie's mother was only about 18 at her birth, the story of a previous marriage seems very unlikely, as does the existence of Marie's supposed half-brothers. Either Marie deliberately manipulated the facts in her memoirs or she was just repeating a story her mother had told her.

Shortly after her daughter's birth, Marie's mother went to live in Bern where she was housekeeper to a Swiss doctor named Philippe Curtius. To aid his work, Curtius made wax models to illustrate human anatomy. Encouraged by the Prince de Conti, a member of the French royal family, he abandoned the medical profession and went to Paris to set up a waxworks.

Once established in the city, Curtius invited Marie's mother to Paris to resume her role as his housekeeper, bringing Marie, by then about 6, with her. This strong commitment to his old housekeeper and her daughter suggests there may have been a deeper relationship between Curtius and the Grosholtzs. Marie always claimed that Curtius was her uncle, but it has been suggested that he was actually her father. Whatever the true circumstances, Curtius treated Marie like a daughter, leading her to claim in her memoirs that he had legally adopted her.

Curtius developed a waxworks exhibition and also fulfilled private commissions, his business benefiting greatly from the Prince de Conti's patronage. He exhibited at local fairs and then set up a permanent exhibition in the Boulevard du Temple, next to Astley's equestrian amphitheatre, where he also lived and had his workshop. Like Madame Tussaud's shows in later years, this exhibition had two separate parts, the first showing wax models of the popular figures of the day and the second – the *Caverne des Grands Voleurs* or Cave of the Great Thieves – displaying waxworks of criminals who had lately been brought to justice. Curtius had discovered a way to profit from the public's morbid fascination with crime, violent punishment and death.

During the 1780s, Curtius ran a second exhibition, the *Salon de Cire*, in the Palais Royal, in the heart of fashionable Paris society. This exhibition was designed as a salon where people could meet each other and walk amongst the waxworks, as if at a highly fashionable gathering. For a smaller fee, customers could just look in from the edge. The central display was the royal family at dinner at Versailles.

Growing up with waxworks

Marie had very little formal education. Curtius taught her how to model in wax and must have been delighted with her aptitude. The models were much simpler than those on display today. The head and hands were made from wax, but the rest of the body was made of wood or straw-stuffed leather, then dressed for display.

Although it was claimed the models were made 'from life', this did not always mean the subject had agreed to sit for a waxwork. Sometimes Curtius and his pupil produced a model from a statue or bust. To make the wax head, a mould had to be created into which the molten wax was poured. Curtius was particularly skilled at mixing different coloured waxes together to produce the correct skin colour – a skill he passed onto Marie. Once the wax had set, the mould was carefully removed and cleaned so that it could be reused to replicate the model or replace it if it was badly damaged or destroyed. The artist then worked on the wax head to remove all trace of the mould and completed it with glass eyes and real hair, one strand at a time. Sometimes they used real teeth as well!

As far as we know, the first wax head that Marie made by herself was that of the famous French writer and philosopher Voltaire in 1778. It is clear that by this time, Marie was a skilled artist and wax modeller in her own right. In her memoirs, she claimed to have taught her skill to Madame Elizabeth, the youngest sister of Louis XVI, and to have lived at Versailles for a number of years.

Modelling in wax was a very fashionable pastime and it is quite likely that Marie did give lessons to the princess. However, there is no official record of her ever having lived at Versailles. This was probably an exaggeration of the truth, to enhance her royal connections in later years.

Curtius did not just teach his young protégée how to make wax models; he taught her to run a business. From Curtius, Marie learned the importance of profit and advertising, how to achieve a more dramatic effect with good lighting, and the importance of keeping the exhibition up to date.

The French Revolution
By 1789, when the events of the French Revolution were beginning to rock Paris, Marie was back living with Curtius in the Boulevard du Temple. According to Marie's memoirs, Curtius entertained many influential people around his dinner table. Again, Marie seems likely to have embellished the truth in order to claim an element of personal relationship with some of the grand people that they modelled. One probably genuine visitor was Benjamin Franklin, as he was known to have a number of waxworks of famous people in his home and it seems reasonable that he acquired these from Curtius. While Curtius claimed that he was a royalist at heart, he took a pro-revolutionary stance in the interests of keeping his family safe. It was also a shrewd business decision

and, as the events of the Revolution unfolded, it was essential for Curtius to keep his displays current.

People flocked to Curtius's exhibition as it gave a visual representation of what was happening in the world around them. Prior to the Revolution, waxworks of the royal family were displayed, seated around a dining table, as they might have been at Versailles. As the Revolution developed, the dining table remained, but the models of the king and queen were replaced by those of revolutionary leaders. At the entrance, the wax doorman greeting visitors changed clothes to reflect the times. The model went from being dressed in royal military uniform to that of the National Guard and then to being dressed as an artisan, 'sans-culottes'.

Occasionally Curtius was away from home and the exhibition fell behind current events and was criticised for displaying the wrong people. When Lafayette's waxwork remained on display after he had fallen from favour, Curtius had to apologise and publicly decapitate the offending figure.

In July 1789, the revolutionaries used two of Curtius's wax heads – those of Necker and the Duke of Orléans – lifted high on poles, to lead their march. One of the heads was completely destroyed in the process. The gruesome reality was that the wax heads were soon replaced by real ones.

Marie was closely involved in the events of the Revolution. When the Bastille was stormed and its governor cruelly murdered, Marie was there soon after, taking a mould of his head. She also made a model of the Comte de Lorges, who had been a prisoner in the Bastille. He had been incarcerated for so long that he couldn't cope with life outside and became something of a symbol of the early Revolution.

After the king and queen and their retinue had been forced to leave Versailles, the new government ordered Curtius to put his models of the royal family on display in the *Petit Trianon*, a small chateau in the palace grounds. Marie was ordered to make casts of the faces of those who had been guillotined, in order to then create wax models. It was often a few hours after the victim had been to the guillotine that poor Marie had to create her mould. She must have had a strong stomach!

One of the leading revolutionaries was a radical journalist and politician named Jean-Paul Marat. In 1793, Charlotte Corder, a young woman from Caen who was opposed to the violent course that the Revolution was taking, came to Paris with the express intention of killing Marat. She stabbed him to death as he took a bath, and was sentenced to death for the crime. Marie made a waxwork of Marat by order of the National Assembly after his assassination. She also made one of Corder, at her own request, before she went to the guillotine. Marat's murder scene was a popular exhibit at the waxworks. At first, people came to mourn Marat's death, but as the Revolution took its course, Corder was hailed as a hero and Marat reviled for the part he had played.

Whilst Curtius was away from home, Marie ran the business. In her memoirs, Marie claimed that during 1794, she and her mother were briefly imprisoned, alongside Josephine, later Napoleon Bonaparte's wife and Empress of France. Although this might have happened, there is no evidence to support her claim. It may have been an attempt to align herself more strongly with the anti-revolutionary cause and boost her reputation through association with the highest ranks of French society.

When Curtius died in September 1794, he left the waxworks exhibition and several properties to Marie. She carried on the business, but it was not very profitable in the years following the French Revolution, as it was difficult to know which waxworks to display. It could prove dangerous to mount exhibits that went against the flow of the political climate.

From 1795, some of Curtius's waxworks went on display in Britain, first in Bond Street, London, and then in various towns around the country, before moving to Baden in modern-day Germany in 1797.

On 16 October 1795, the 33-year-old Marie married François Tussaud, a civil engineer several years her junior. It is hard to tell what motivated the marriage, which doesn't appear to have been a great success. It seems she was wary of her husband from the start as, by her marriage settlement, Marie retained control of her own property – an unusual arrangement for the time. In France, as in Britain, a woman's property normally passed to her husband when she married.

The next five years were extremely challenging for Marie. She gave birth to her first child, Marie, in 1796 and then had to endure the grief of losing her as a baby. Marie made a waxwork of her daughter, which she later put on display. Two years later, Joseph was born, followed by another son, Francis, in 1800. Marie's mother and aunt lived with her and helped look after the children, but if she had hoped for support from her husband in running the business, she was to be disappointed. François was better at spending money than earning it, losing heavily through poor investments in theatre property.

The waxworks go to London

In 1802, Marie had the opportunity to take her waxworks to England. With the signing of the Treaty of Amiens, France was at peace with the United Kingdom, for a while at least. Paul Philipstal was a fellow exhibitor in Paris who ran a phantasmagoria magic lantern show. He planned to take his exhibition to London and offered Marie the option of joining him. Marie jumped at the chance. This seemed like the perfect opportunity to restore the family fortunes and perhaps give her some relief from an unsatisfactory marriage.

Marie entered into a partnership with Philipstal. He agreed to pay for all the travel and advertising costs in return for half of Marie's profits. Leaving her infant son with her mother and aunt, Marie travelled to England with her 4-year-old son Joseph and around thirty wax models, a number of smaller waxworks that Curtius had made, and all the casts. They set up their shows in the Lyceum Theatre in London where they ran for the whole season.

Rather than use her own name, Marie decided to build on the reputation of Curtius's waxworks, some of which had toured Britain a few years previously. The public was therefore invited to see Curtius's Cabinet of Curiosities, not Madame Tussaud's waxworks.

It did not take Marie long to realise that Philipstal was not a reliable partner. He had failed to include her show in any of the advertisements and did not pay for all the travel costs as promised. In addition, some of her models had been damaged in the crossing and she had to repair them herself, whilst struggling with a language she did not know and looking after a 4-year-old boy. It would be an understatement to say that Marie had her hands full.

Marie had learned from Curtius how to profit from the public's enthusiasm for the macabre. From the start, the touring exhibition comprised two sections – the main exhibition of waxworks and a room dedicated to the exhibits which we would now associate with the Chamber of Horrors, a nickname given to Marie's 'Adjoining Room' by the magazine *Punch* in 1846.

The main exhibition included the glamorous figures of the French royal family, which Curtius had carefully stored away during the Revolution, as well as Emperor Napoleon and Josephine. The other section included gruesome reminders of the French Revolution, like Marat being murdered in his bath and the heads of victims of the guillotine. Marie soon added British criminals to her exhibition, such as Colonel Edward Despard, who was executed in 1803 for plotting to murder George III.

Marie charged an extra sixpence for entrance to this room, which she advertised as a separate exhibition: 'The following highly interesting figures & objects, in consequence of the peculiarity of their appearance, are placed in an adjoining room, and form a separate exhibition, well worthy the inspection of artists and amateurs. Admittance to the above, 6d.'[1]

Throughout this time, Marie wrote home to her husband every week, giving detailed accounts of how well the exhibition was doing, as if trying to justify the course she had taken. She was always very affectionate towards her younger son, urging her husband to look after him, as well as taking care of her mother and aunt, and she talked about her eventual return to France. Marie complained that she received very few letters in return.

Meanwhile, François was not faring very well in Paris. Struggling to run the business, he demanded that Marie return home, but she refused. Marie decided to transfer all her French property over to her husband, but declined to send him any of the money she was currently earning, claiming that she was barely surviving.

Waxworks on tour
When the London season finished in April 1803, both Marie's waxwork exhibition and Philipstal's magic lantern show relocated to Scotland. This was a politic move, as France was once more at war with Britain and there were some restrictions on the movements of non-British subjects. It was a costly move for Marie. She sent her models up by sea and, once more, several of them were damaged. Philipstal also let her down again, failing to cover all the costs and leaving Marie decidedly out of pocket.

However, it was worth the effort. Marie planned the opening of her exhibition to coincide with the Edinburgh horse show and the city was heaving with people. With her keen eye for profit, she charged the exorbitant entry fee of two shillings – twice the usual rate for this type of entertainment – during the horse show. When that event was over, she reduced the price to the regular one shilling admittance. As always, Marie kept a detailed record of her receipts and expenditure and was delighted with her profits. Her exhibition in Edinburgh was a great success. In fact, it was much more successful than her business partner's and Marie was aggrieved at handing over half her profits to Philipstal.

For the first time, Marie issued a brochure to accompany her exhibition – an innovative idea which she repeated at every new venue. At sixpence a copy, Marie had found an opportunity to extract even more money from her customers. The brochure included brief biographical details to accompany the models, promoting it as an educational experience. Some factual details were not entirely accurate, but it did provide some background to the characters exhibited in wax. From Edinburgh, the exhibition moved to Glasgow and then to Ireland. In about 1804, Marie bought herself out of the Philipstal partnership. It was probably no coincidence that around the same time, her letters home suddenly stopped. There was no more talk of going back to France. Having just managed to extricate herself from a partnership with one unsatisfactory man, she had no intention of submitting herself to another.

If Marie returned to Paris, she knew that she would be subject to the Code Civil that had come in since the Revolution and all her income would belong to her financially inept husband. Marie had already proved that she could manage very well as an independent woman and she was not about to lose that freedom. Even if she had gone back, there was nowhere for her exhibition to go, as her husband had given up the Paris waxworks.

Now confidently independent, Marie started to exhibit in her own name from 1808. She took her exhibition back to Scotland and then toured all over England. Marie was a very astute businesswoman. She only toured big towns and cities where there were lots of upper- and middle-class people who would be willing to pay to see the waxworks. In addition, she planned her touring schedule to coincide with local events, such as horse races, when the town would be packed with potential customers. She always tried to hire the local assembly rooms or a theatre or town hall for her exhibition. Although her schedule was planned, the start and finish dates in each place were flexible, and always dictated by how the receipts were going. If takings were up, she would extend the stay; if the entry numbers fell, she would move on.

Then as now, royalty was always popular with the crowd. To the French royal family, Marie added waxworks of George III and Queen Charlotte, together with those of George, Prince of Wales, and his wife, Princess Caroline. Marie also modelled royals from history, including

Elizabeth I and her unfortunate cousin Mary, Queen of Scots. She added British heroes, such as Admiral Horatio Lord Nelson, who had defeated the French at the Battle of Trafalgar in 1805, and popular characters like actress Sarah Siddons.

Scandalous characters always drew good crowds. When the Mrs Clarke scandal blew up in 1809, Marie was quick to model her and put the waxwork on display. Mary Anne Clarke, ex-mistress of George III's second son, Frederick, Duke of York, was accused of selling army promotions for cash. She claimed that the duke had known what was going on and, though cleared, he was forced to resign as Commander-in-Chief of the armed forces. The Scottish public flocked to see the face of the woman who had caused so much trouble. In addition to the exhibition, Marie earned money through private commissions. With her love of royal patronage, Marie was thrilled when Frederica, Duchess of York, commissioned two waxworks. The duchess allowed Marie to use her name on the advertisements for her exhibition.

After the Battle of Waterloo, the public was fascinated not only with the hero, the Duke of Wellington, but also with his adversary, Napoleon Bonaparte. There was a waxwork of Napoleon in Marie's original show but, in 1815, she made a new one. While Napoleon was in a ship anchored in Portsmouth, Marie cleverly staged a massive publicity stunt by arranging to go on board and model his face before he left for exile on St Helena.

Marie's son Joseph grew up with the waxworks business as his mother had done before him and he learned to model in wax. From 1813, when he was about 15, he took an active part in the business. He played piano with a little orchestra which provided background music and learned to make silhouettes which Marie sold as a cheap alternative to those who could not afford to buy their own wax model.

Although Marie claimed affection for the infant son she had left behind in France, she made no attempt to see Francis and missed his entire childhood. According to family legend, aged 17, Francis came to England to join his mother and brother, but was met with the news that they had been lost at sea crossing over from Ireland along with all her waxworks. Clearly the news was false and they had survived, but it sent Francis scurrying back to Paris. It wasn't until four years later that Francis finally joined his mother in England and started to learn how to make waxworks.

From around 1820, art galleries became very popular and Marie responded by adding more paintings and memorabilia to her exhibition, making it more like a museum. One of the strengths of Marie's exhibition was how she clothed her models. Wherever possible, she dressed them in clothes that had actually belonged to the subject, which had either been bought or donated by the person. Marie added a tableau of George IV's coronation of 1821 and later managed to buy the actual robes he wore to use in her display.

A popular addition to the second room was the body-snatching murder duo, Burke and Hare. They resorted to killing their unsuspecting lodgers in order to provide corpses that they could sell for medical research. Burke was convicted of murder and executed in 1829. Marie modelled Burke during the trial whilst her sons completed Hare. They also obtained a cast of Burke's head after the execution.

A permanent home for the waxworks
When the waxworks returned to London in 1833, it was not with the intention of settling there permanently. The exhibition was growing and becoming more elaborate, however, and transport costs were increasing. Marie was getting old, and her two sons had eleven children between them. The rail network was making it easier for visitors to get to the exhibition rather than the exhibition having to travel to them.

These were all contributing factors in Marie's decision to establish a permanent base, but ultimately it all came down to profit. Marie took short leases, for a few months at a time, ready to move on as soon as takings fell. From 1835, the exhibition was based at the 'Bazaar, Baker Street, Portman Square'[2] a site near to all the main railway terminals.

Then, in 1836, Marie made a waxwork of Maria Malibran, a popular young Spanish opera singer who had died suddenly. Myriads of visitors flocked to see the new waxwork which Marie had advertised widely. Takings doubled in a single week, persuading Marie to stay in London. Initially, Marie continued to take short leases, always ready to move on if the profits dipped.

Again, with an eye on profit, Marie spotted an opportunity to sell refreshments to her exhibition visitors. She set up a place for people to buy soft drinks and food in between the main exhibition and the 'Separate Room' – the modern-day Chamber of Horrors.

Once the exhibition was settled at Baker Street, Marie started building up her display of Napoleonic memorabilia. She purchased items that had belonged to Napoleon when they came up for sale and in this way amassed the largest collection of Napoleonic ephemera anywhere in the world. This included his coronation robes and the carriage he had abandoned after the Battle of Waterloo.

Queen Victoria valued the good publicity that the waxworks exhibition gave her and allowed exact copies of her robes to be made for a tableau of her coronation. She also gave Marie permission to order a replica of her wedding dress for using in a tableau of her wedding in 1840. During the years following Prince Albert's death, the waxworks gave people a way to see their somewhat reclusive queen. There is no doubt that Madame Tussaud's waxwork displays helped maintain Queen Victoria's popularity.

The last years

Marie published her memoirs in 1838, with the help of a family friend, Francis Hervé. These memoirs pitched Marie as the intimate friend of the French royal family, helping to establish her position in society as something rather higher than it really was.

By 1840, the waxworks began to be known by the name Madame Tussaud and Sons, recognising the part that Marie's sons now played, making new waxworks and helping to run the business. When Marie's husband realised how successful her exhibition had become, he made one final attempt to extort money from her. He sent a friend to England in 1841 to act on his behalf, but was met with the news that his wife had put her money out of his reach by transferring the ownership of the business to her sons.

Some visitors to the exhibition in 1840 wrote: 'We saw a wax-work figure of Madame Tussaud herself in the exhibition, and when we saw her alive upon leaving the room, we could scarce discover the real from the imitation.'[3]

Marie made her last known waxwork – a model of herself – in 1842. Although her sons were now largely in control, Marie remained involved in the business up until a few months before her death. Marie Tussaud died on 15 April 1850 and was buried in the Roman Catholic chapel in Chelsea.

Marie's legacy

Madame Tussaud's waxworks was neither the first nor the only such entertainment in London, but it is the only one to have survived into the twenty-first century. Its longevity was largely due to Marie's entrepreneurial abilities. Throughout her life she kept a tight rein on the business finances and always made decisions based on profit. She kept the waxworks up to date, marketed her exhibition well and pitched it as a safe, educational, family entertainment.

In 1884, the waxworks exhibition moved to a new purpose-built site on Marylebone Road – the same site that it stands on today. In 1925, the Tussaud building was gutted by fire, destroying almost everything on display including George IV's coronation robes and all the Napoleonic relics. During the Second World War, Tussaud's suffered further losses in a bombing raid in 1940. Financial difficulties led to the business passing out of family control. But despite all this, Madame Tussaud's survived and remains one of London's top tourist attractions, visited by millions of tourists every year. There are now Madame Tussaud's attractions all over the world.

Marie made the Tussaud name so famous that even when the business went out of the family, the waxworks kept the name Madame Tussaud – a memorial to possibly the greatest female entrepreneur of her time.

Chapter 5

The Benevolent Mountaineer – Mary Parminter (1767–1849)

Mary Parminter may have been a country girl born into a wealthy Devonshire family, but that did not mean that she obeyed the rules of fashionable Georgian society. At that time, mountain climbing, science, property ownership and foreign travel were generally the province of men. Not only did Mary do all these with little or no male support, throughout her life and beyond, she actively promoted the rights of women.

Her legacy into the twenty-first century is the Mary Parminter Trust, a charity that continues to provide homes for those in need, particularly women. Mary also left her mark with A la Ronde, the unique sixteen-sided house in Exmouth that she built with her cousin Jane, now owned by the National Trust.

Mary's tale is that of a woman who broke with the mould of her time, allowing her beliefs and her determination to continue making a real difference to the lives of people today.

Early life

Born in 1767 in Barnstaple, Devon, Mary was the eldest child of Richard Parminter and Mary 'Polly' Walrond. The Parminter family were successful merchants, having built a fortune from trade with the Americas and the West Indies. Richard's marriage to Polly Walrond provided an advantageous connection to another prosperous, non-conformist family whose wealth would eventually pass to his daughter Mary. Richard had been called to the Bar and was a counsellor in law. This was a socially prestigious role involving work in the superior courts and was an acceptable profession for an upper class gentleman.

The Parminters were devout Christians, worshipping at the Independent Chapel in Cross Street where Mary was baptised on 11

March 1767. Little is known about Mary's early life. Her younger sister Rebecca was born in 1768 and another sister Harriet was born two years later but did not survive infancy.

In April 1772, further tragedy struck. Mary's mother died leaving Richard Parminter with two small daughters to look after. The grief-stricken Richard was clearly unable to cope, as the following year he sent 6-year-old Mary and little Rebecca to stay with his uncle, John Parminter, in Braunton, Devon. John's four children – Jane, Mary Ann, Elizabeth and John – had also just lost their mother.

The influence of cousin Jane

Whilst living together in the same household, an enduring friendship developed between Mary Parminter and her cousins and particularly with the eldest, Jane. In those early years, Jane, seventeen years older than Mary, must have been a mother-like figure to her young cousins. Jane had been born into another branch of the wealthy Parminter family. At the time of her birth on 5 February 1750, her parents, John and Jane Parminter, were living in Lisbon where her father was a successful merchant. John traded mainly in Portuguese wine and had built a bottling facility in Lisbon.

On 1 November 1755, when Jane was aged 5, the Great Lisbon Earthquake devastated the city, killing thousands of people and causing a massive tsunami. Fortunately, the Parminters were unharmed as they were visiting England at the time, but John's business was completely destroyed. A true entrepreneur, John realised that there would be a huge demand for materials to rebuild the city, and successfully restored his business fortunes by diversifying into quick drying cement. It would appear that he was no longer willing to risk the lives of his young family in Lisbon, however; Jane and her younger siblings remained in Devon while their father travelled to and from Portugal.

In 1779, when Mary was 12 and still living with Jane and her other Parminter cousins, news arrived that her father had died. Richard's death transformed Mary and Rebecca into heiresses, with rights to considerable estates when they came of age. Richard left Mary his estate in Ottery St Mary and his 'picture set in diamonds',[1] whilst he left Larkbeare House and gardens and her mother's watch and rings to Rebecca. The remainder was placed in trust for them in equal shares until they came of age. A year later, their cousin Jane, now aged 30, also became an heiress when her father died. Mary and Rebecca and their Parminter cousins went to London to live with Jane's married sister, Mary Ann and her husband George Frend, in Greville Street. A lovely memento remains of this time when Jane and her siblings were together in London. An exquisite silhouette picture of the family was drawn by the French artist Francis Torond in 1783, which is on display in the drawing room of A la Ronde. The ink drawing depicts George and Mary Ann Frend, together with Jane, Elizabeth and John, in silhouette, and includes some wonderful details like a squirrel sitting on the table. However, Mary is not in the picture. Neither is her sister Rebecca who died that year, quite possibly before the silhouette was drawn.

At the age of 16, Mary was now the sole heiress of her father's estates and could be confident of being financially independent for life.

The Parminter ladies' Grand Tour
It must have been during this time in London that Jane and her sister Elizabeth concocted their plans to travel on the continent. They were both wealthy, independent women having inherited the equivalent of half a million pounds between them on the death of their father. Money was no object and clearly foreign travel was more appealing than getting married. It is unsurprising that young Mary Parminter, having lost both her parents and her sister, should cling to her cousins and be influenced by their adventurous ambitions.

It was certainly unusual for single women to make the Grand Tour, especially without a man to lead the party. Making the Grand Tour was predominantly a male activity, often a coming-of-age ritual. Young gentlemen finished their education by travelling on the continent, experiencing life in other nations and visiting the cultural centres of Europe, particularly Paris and Rome. The Grand Tour was also seen as a way of allowing young gentlemen to sow their wild oats a long way from home where they would not cause any embarrassment to their parents. Typically, the Grand Tour took about two years and the travellers would acquire souvenirs along the way – classical statues, a portrait by one of the fashionable artists like Pompeo Batoni, and paintings of what they had seen.

Jane was no stranger to travel. She had been born in Lisbon and may have travelled in Europe whilst her father was active in his business concerns there. No doubt she had talked about her experiences abroad and stirred up a desire in Elizabeth and Mary to have their own adventures. There may have been a desire to follow her brother John, who had left for France shortly after the Torond ink drawing was made. Like his father before him, John was a merchant. A passport issued some years later suggests that John was in Naples at the same time as his sisters. Jane was certainly not afraid of travelling and had plenty of money with which to indulge her desire to explore.

On 23 June 1784, Jane, Elizabeth and Mary left Dover for the continent, accompanied by another lady, possibly a Miss Colville. Jane kept a journal of their travels, which may have given us a complete record of where they visited, but, frustratingly, the original was destroyed during the Exeter Blitz of 1942 during the Second World War.

All that remains is a partial transcription of the early weeks of their tour which was published by a distant cousin, the Reverend Oswald Reichel, in 1902. According to the extract, the ladies visited Abbeville, Chantilly and Paris including a visit to Versailles.

Jane described the hall of mirrors:

The grand gallery is noble 17 windows in front, opposite each window is a looking glass of the same size. She went on to say: *We saw the King a corpulent man not strikingly agreeable. The Queen is tall & elegant small features. The gardens are very large full of Water & Trees but not so gay with Flowers. There are most delightful statues full of expression. The Menagery is very good.*[2]

They visited the park at St Cloud, the Tuileries Gardens, Les Invalides and the Gobelins tapestry factory. They travelled through the Fontainebleau Forest and visited the botanical gardens in Dijon. Jane wrote: 'Went to the Academy of Arts and sciences, saw the busts of all the great men of Dijon and the living geniuses who sat round the Table. M Morveau who went up in the Ballon [sic] talk'd upon Chemistry, two or 3 othrs on Natural History & Poetry.'[3]

Where the party travelled after this, and exactly how long they were abroad, is subject to considerable debate. Family tradition says they were in Marseille in southern France in May 1785. A later family member was adamant that the ladies visited the Basilica of San Vitale in Ravenna in Italy and that this was the inspiration for the unusual design of their future home at A la Ronde. The roads to Ravenna were so bad at this time that if they had gone there, then they almost certainly journeyed there by boat from Venice.

Souvenirs give clues as to where the ladies visited including a print of the tomb of Madame Langhans near Berne in Switzerland – a popular eighteenth century tourist site. Their large collection of Piranesi prints suggests that they visited and liked Rome. There is also a print of the ancient bridge at Narni in Umbria in central Italy – one of the largest Roman bridges ever built.

A shell picture of Isola Bella, an island in Lake Maggiore in northern Italy, has Mary's handwriting on the back. The Borromeo family had transformed their rocky island into a 'pyramid of flower-laden terraces'[4] in the seventeenth century, and built the Borromeo Palace. American writer Edith Wharton called it 'one of the most important sights of the "grand tour".'[5]

Of particular interest to the Parminters was the shell grotto:

The beautiful series of rooms in the south basement, opening on the gardens, and decorated with the most exquisite ornamentation of pebble-work and seashells, mingled with delicately tinted stucco. These low vaulted rooms, with marble floors, grotto-like walls, and fountains dripping into fluted conchs, are like a poet's notion of some twilight refuge from summer heats, where the languid green air has the coolness of water.[6]

This sight must have left a deep impression on Jane and Mary, years later inspiring their own marvellously decorated Shell Gallery at A la Ronde.

Pioneering female mountaineers

A group of single women travelling in Europe was unusual enough in the late eighteenth century, but the Parminter ladies were not satisfied with just visiting the popular tourist sites; they wanted to climb mountains. Their achievement was so significant that it was recorded in contemporary journals.

An excerpt from *L'Espri des Journaux* in December 1786 said:

Three English ladies (Miss Parminter) also climbed this summer the Buet glacier led by Monsieur Berenger and the guide named the great Jorasse. They had to travel through four hours of snow before reaching the summit; but they were seasoned by two hundred miles of walking in the Alps of Switzerland and Vallais.[7]

The implication is that not only did Mary, Jane and Elizabeth climb *Mont Buet*, but that they were experienced mountain walkers, having walked, according to the article, 200 miles in the Swiss and Vallais Alps.

Le Buet or *Mont Buet* is a glacier with a peak of 3,096m altitude, and the Parminter sisters are generally credited with being the first women to climb above 3,000m. No mention is made of the fourth lady who set out with them for Europe and so it is assumed that she had already left their party by this time.

Return to England
There is no record of exactly how long the Parminter ladies were travelling in Europe. It was at least two, and probably as many as four years, but by October 1788 at least one of them, Elizabeth, was back in London. Unwell, she had returned to make her will and it is unlikely she came back alone. She died in 1791, and Jane is recorded as being in London to be granted probate.

By now, Mary was a very rich woman. In addition to the fortune she had received from her father when she came of age in 1788, she had inherited a second fortune from her mother's Walrond relatives. As an eye-wateringly wealthy 24-year-old in late Georgian England, it seems impossible to believe that Mary was not pursued by younger sons of the aristocracy, desperate to achieve their own financial independence by marrying money. Presumably, if she had chosen to, Mary could have made a very advantageous marriage. But she did not. Perhaps Mary had grown to prize her independence too much to submit her will to that of a husband.

Mary could, perhaps, have acquired a title and a magnificent home. But at the same time, by marrying, she would have passed control of her wealth to her husband. The terms in which some of the bequests in her will are couched suggest that she was fully aware of the power a husband had over his wife and her possessions. While we cannot know exactly what motivated Mary to remain single, there are clues scattered through what we know of her life. Perhaps the most significant is that her cousin Jane, the single greatest influence in her life after the death of her mother, also chose not to go to the altar.

Back in 1769, when she was 19, and before Mary had come to live with her, Jane was sent to stay with her Aunt Margaret and her husband, Philip Hurlock, who lived near St Paul's in London, where her uncle practised as a surgeon at St Bartholomew's Hospital. It seems likely that Jane's parents intended that she should take her place in society and find a husband. Something prevented this. Jane was set to inherit a substantial amount of money from her parents and so it seems unlikely that she would have received no offers for her hand. Did she have an unhappy love affair that put her off marriage or was she so afraid of the dangers of childbirth that she did not dare to get married? Coming from a strong Christian family, was she so committed to her faith that she chose celibacy so that her devotion to God would not be diminished by having to care for a husband and family? Or was she simply not interested in a heterosexual relationship?

We cannot underestimate the Hurlocks' influence on Jane during these formative years. The Hurlocks belonged to the Moravian church and Philip was listed as an active member of the Society for the Furtherance of the Gospel, suggesting that he took his faith very seriously. Jane would have attended the Moravian chapel in Fetter Lane with them and been influenced by their theology. The Moravians were very forward-thinking in their attitude towards women. They believed that women were spiritually equal to men and expected women to act as spiritual leaders. It is impossible to assess how much this would have affected Jane's thinking on the position of women in society. Jane also learned several languages and may have travelled in Europe with her aunt and uncle. It seems likely that she acquired her love of science from her uncle, who was elected a member of the Royal Society in 1780.

Jane returned home to Devon in 1773 when her mother died. Aged 23, she was well-educated, devoutly Christian, unmarried and, undoubtedly, had very strong opinions about the value of female independence. Within weeks, her 6-year-old cousin Mary came into her household, and under her influence. That influence can only have deepened during the years of travelling together on the Grand Tour. There can be little doubt that Mary's later advocacy of the status of the single woman was deeply rooted in her relationship with her cousin.

By 1793, Mary's home was in south Devon, where the majority of her relatives resided. She lived in Kenton, a small village in Devon dominated by Powderham Castle, just across the river from Exmouth. Jane was almost certainly living with her. As neither lady was disposed to get married and pass the management of their worldly wealth into the hands of men, they decided to build a house in which they could live together permanently.

They bought some land in the parish of Withycombe Raleigh in Exmouth, known as Great Courtlands, and started to build A la Ronde. Although the journey from where they were living in Kenton to Withycombe Raleigh would have been tortuous by road, it was only a ferry ride across the river from Kenton to Lympstone, and then about a mile by road to the site of their new home.

The creation of A la Ronde

A la Ronde is not the house that most wealthy people would have built in the Georgian period. It is not a Palladian mansion, but of an unusual design and a very modest size. It was reputedly inspired by the octagonal Basilica of San Vitale in Ravenna, visited on the Grand Tour. However, A la Ronde is not, as might be expected from its supposed inspiration, a building of eight sides, but of sixteen.

The house was designed to make the best possible use of natural illumination. Every window was set on a join between two walls to let in the maximum amount of light. The main rooms were placed around a central octagonal hall with doors leading from one room into the next via tiny lobbies so that you could walk right around the house without having to cross the hall. Jane and Mary enjoyed the early morning sun in their bedrooms and then moved around the house with the light as the day progressed.

Jane and Mary clearly loved living here. They filled the rooms with mementoes from their travels, covering the walls with prints and shell pictures that they had bought during their Grand Tour.

They also used their creative skills to decorate their home. You can still see the results of their labours today. The drawing room has an exquisite border made of feathers, which miraculously survived later alterations to the house when two rooms were knocked together. There are two work tables on display in the drawing room which have been inlaid by hand. On the walls are numerous silhouettes, many of which were made by Jane and Mary and other members of the Parminter family.

The most astounding legacy to Jane and Mary's industry is the Shell Gallery at the top of A la Ronde. Inspired by the grotto of the Borromeo

73

Palace in Italy, the two cousins constructed a giant mosaic – made not just of shells, but of all manner of items including feathers, stones and paintings. The gallery fills the whole of the room inside the roof of the house, overlooking the octagonal hall below. This fragile creation, which still survives, embodies the spirit of freedom and independence exhibited by the two ladies.

The creation of the Point in View Chapel
As active non-conformist Christians, Jane and Mary worshipped at the Glenorchy Independent Chapel in Exeter Road, Exmouth. But there was a problem. Jane and Mary liked to attend church regularly and it was not always easy to travel into Exmouth during the winter months when the roads were bad. They decided to build a chapel on their own land near A la Ronde. The chapel was completed in 1811, at the very start of the Regency, but on 6 November, before the first service was held, Jane died. Her body was interred in the vault underneath the chapel.

The chapel was named 'Point in View'. An odd name for a chapel, but it is thought to reflect Jane and Mary's Protestant beliefs and in particular, their desire to see Jews converted to Christianity. The Bishop of Exeter gave his blessing on 3 February 1812, allowing the chapel to be used for non-conformist public worship.

The Mary Parminter Charity
It was Jane and Mary's vision to establish more than just a chapel at Point in View. Wealth had allowed them to live as independent women. Their desire was to enable future generations of women to enjoy something of that same independence. To this end, on 10 May 1813, the Mary Parminter Charity was created with an initial bequest from Mary of £1,000 of bank stock.

The trust deed laid out Mary's stipulations for the operation of the chapel, almshouses and school. Point in View was to provide a home for the minister of the church who was to be a Protestant dissenter – a married man with no children.

The other apartments in the building were to be occupied by four single women 'of good character, possessed of some small independent property' who were 'industriously engaged in plain work, knitting and spinning'.[8] The women had to be at least 50 years old and be spinsters rather than widows, and preference was to be given to Jewesses who had converted to Christianity. One of these women was to be appointed as schoolmistress to teach the six poor girls given places at the school by the trustees.

Two collecting boxes were placed inside the chapel – one for the minister and one for the Society for Promoting Christianity among the Jews. Mary gave annual gifts of clothing and educational books to the poor children being educated in the school.

Mary's last years

Very little is known about how Mary passed the years after Jane's death. She continued to live at A la Ronde with just a few servants and the 1841 census shows she was living with Elizabeth Lavington, whom she described in her will as 'my dear friend and Cousin'.[9]

Mary died on 18 December 1849 at the age of 82 after a short illness, and was interred with her cousin Jane in the vault beneath the Point in View Chapel on 27 December. The trustees of the Mary Parminter Charity recorded in their minute book that Mary was 'distinguished for intelligent generosity, simplicity and uprightness' and further that she was 'a generous friend of good men and Christian ministers and an unsolicitous promoter of Protestant and Catholic Christianity.' They wrote that she had led 'so useful and endeared a life' and had 'accomplished a large amount of good and acquired an exemplary and enduring reputation.'[10]

Mary's will

Mary's will is an incredibly long document which, in its detail, further evidences her commitment to the status of single women.

This is startlingly evident in her treatment of her home. Mary was passionate about A la Ronde and wanted her beloved home to be preserved in its existing state. She intended that A la Ronde should be 'held and enjoyed as a convenient and delightful residue for a kinswoman who shall not have been married.'[9] Mary left her home to a number of single ladies in her family in succession. If the lady in line to inherit should marry, or die, or break any of the conditions of the bequest, then the house was to pass to the next lady in line. The conditions were that they should not change anything or let it out.

Amongst the personal bequests there are some lines that remind us of Mary's concern for the position of women. For example, in a bequest to Richard Parminter Melhuish for his lifetime, and then to his daughter

Mary, and then to her eldest child, Mary specifies that the money should pass to the eldest child 'whether son or daughter'.[9] But perhaps the most telling lines are after a long list of bequests to family members and friends, ministers and their wives. Mary stipulated that 'such of the aforesaid legacies as are bequeathed to married women shall be paid into their own proper hands or to such person or persons as they may appoint for their respective separated use and not be subject to the control or engagements of their respective husbands'.[9] Even after her death, Mary was busy promoting the right of women to own property.

Others benefiting from Mary's will included various missionary societies including the Moravian Brethren Missions, the Bible Society and the London Missionary Society, as well as several societies working with Jews, including the London Society for Promoting Christianity among the Jews. Money was also left to the Exeter Female Penitentiary and the Gipsy Asylum and Industrial School near Blandford.

Mary's legacy
Today, as in her own lifetime, few people have heard of Mary Parminter. Yet she, and her cousin Jane, demonstrated and advocated the freedom and independence of women, in defiance of the expectations of late Georgian England. Moreover, Mary channelled her independent spirit into a legacy that has lasted into the twenty-first century, in the form of her trust.

Mary's charity still continues its work today, though perhaps not quite as she had imagined. Her school for girls closed in 1901 after a visit from the Education Authorities deemed that it was not a 'Certified Efficient School'.

Despite her stipulation in the trust deed that the plan of the building should not be altered, the charity was given permission to adapt the accommodation for modern requirements. New cottages were built in the 1960s and a second group in the 1970s. The rooms in the Point in View Chapel were adapted for the use of the church, with a kitchen and a meeting room as well as improved accommodation for one resident. The rules for the residents have changed, but the charity continues to operate and is affiliated to the Almshouses Association.

For many years, A la Ronde served Mary's intended purpose as a home for unmarried women in her family. It was inherited in turn by three of her cousins – Jane Hurlock, Sophia Hurlock and Stella Reichel. It was never Mary's intention that a man should possess A la Ronde, but in 1880, it passed into the ownership of Stella's brother, Oswald Reichel.

Oswald made changes. He put in central heating, added extra windows and knocked two of the rooms and the intervening lobby into one in order to create a larger drawing room. He would probably have known Mary as a boy and heard about their adventures from his father, and he obviously held Jane and Mary Parminter in great esteem. In his will, Oswald attempted to make provision for A la Ronde to stay within the family, but his widow tried to sell the property for development. Quite by chance, Oswald's niece, Margaret Tudor, spotted that A la Ronde was for sale and bought it at auction in 1929. With her sister Stella, she opened it to the public for the first time.

Legal battles over ownership almost ruined the two sisters. They fought courageously to keep A la Ronde intact, selling off land and trying to persuade first the National Trust, and then the Mary Parminter Charity, to take it on. Finally, in 1991, A la Ronde was bought with a grant from the National Heritage Memorial Fund and passed into the care of the National Trust, thus preserving Mary's legacy in perpetuity.

Mary Parminter blazed a quiet yet remarkable trail. She is recognised as one of the earliest female mountaineers and she was a woman of science, with a microscope, a telescope and a camera obscura being listed in her will.

Most remarkable of all, Mary fiercely defended her own status as an independent woman, while also seeking to allow other women to enjoy similar freedom in the generations that came after her.

Chapter 6

Mother of Historical Fiction – Maria Edgeworth (1768–1849)

Many of us love a good historical novel that reinvigorates the past through powerful storytelling, weaving a fictional tale into a real historical setting. Historical fiction, in its modern form, all began with the work of one of the most popular authors in Regency Britain, Maria Edgeworth. Her novel, *Castle Rackrent*, is generally considered to be the first historical novel. Before her, people had written about historical characters and they had written stories, but she was the first to write a popular novel based on fictional characters in a historical context.

Early life

Maria owed her very existence to an event that has become a staple of so many historical romance novels – an elopement to Gretna Green. In a flush of emotional excitement, her father, Richard Lovell Edgeworth, an inventor and educationalist from a family of Irish landowners, rushed north of the border with Anna Maria Elers. It was an infatuation and perhaps, even as he stood before the anvil in the blacksmith's cottage at Gretna, Richard wondered whether he was doing the right thing.

The couple's first daughter, Maria, was born at her grandfather's house in Black Bourton in Oxfordshire on New Year's Day 1768.[1] Perhaps by now her father regretted the impulse that had led him into an unequal marriage. Anna Maria was not his intellectual equal and when he met the embodiment of his ideal woman in the person of Honora Sneyd, he struggled to face the inadequacies of his wife. Leaving Maria and her two younger sisters with their mother, he took his son and went to Lyons, in France, where he was occupied building bridges.

He did not return until released from his marriage by the death of Maria's mother in 1773 when Maria was just 5 years old. Within six months, Richard had married Honora Sneyd. Thoroughly taken up with his new wife, Richard had little time to spare for his daughters. Maria was labelled as difficult, and when her stepmother became ill, Maria was sent to Mrs Lattafiere's school in Derby where she gained a reputation for storytelling to amuse the other pupils.

In 1780, life in the Edgeworth household changed again. Honora died of consumption and within a year, Richard had married her sister, Elizabeth Sneyd.

Richard Edgeworth's closest friend was Thomas Day. They had known one another for many years and shared literary interests. Day was responsible for an incident that almost ruined Maria's literary career before it had even started. Whilst visiting his home in Anningsley in Surrey when she was about 13 years old, Maria suffered from an eye complaint. Day jeopardised Maria's future career by his well-meaning attempts to cure this by applying tar water to her eyes. As result of this misguided medical intervention, poor Maria was nearly blinded. Fortunately, her eyes recovered.

Whilst Maria's vision was on the mend, her father encouraged her to study arithmetic as it didn't require so much use of the eyes. This knowledge proved very useful when she was given the chance to help her father manage his estate after the family relocated to Ireland in 1782.

They moved to an estate in County Longford her father had inherited some years before, appropriately named Edgeworthstown. It was the place that Maria was to call home for the rest of her life. The Edgeworthstown estate had been badly managed and needed a lot of work to put it into order.

It was around the time of this move that Richard discovered in Maria a quickness that raised a new interest in his hitherto-neglected eldest daughter, and Maria responded eagerly. Maria accompanied her father on his visits around the estate and acted as his rent clerk. A new bond grew up between them that would be maintained for the rest of his life.

The Edgeworths were landowners and people of consequence in Ireland. Maria had an active social life and was on visiting terms with all the local gentry. She was particularly friendly with the Pakenhams – Thomas Pakenham, Earl of Longford, and his family, including his sister, Kitty Pakenham, who married the Duke of Wellington. She also had a close relationship with her father's sister, Mrs Ruxton, and her daughters, who lived at Black Castle.

As the eldest daughter, Maria helped to bring up the increasing number of young Edgeworths from all of her father's marriages. There is no doubt that she was a very capable young woman. In 1791, she was left in Ireland with most of the children whilst Richard and Elizabeth visited Clifton in Bristol, England. They wrote to Maria requesting her to join them, and she managed the journey from Ireland to Clifton accompanied by all of the little Edgeworths in her care.

Maria's early gift of storytelling was put to good use entertaining her younger siblings. They were a ready audience for her tales and helped her to easily gauge the success of each story that she wrote. In 1796, she gathered her most popular stories into a volume of tales for children – *The Parent's Assistant*. As the title implies, these were in part educational, with a strong moral tone. Interestingly, some people thought her work irreligious because she taught good character without any reference whatsoever to the Christian faith.

Letters for Literary Ladies

This children's story book was quite different from Maria's first publication – *Letters for Literary Ladies* – which had come out the previous year. *Letters for Literary Ladies* was a spirited defence for the education of women. The catalyst for this work was no doubt the dogmatic attitude of her father's friend, Thomas Day, with which she firmly differed. Despite disagreeing with Day's views, it is very clear from her father's memoirs, the second volume of which she wrote, that Maria held him in great respect.

Day had very strong opinions about both the position of women as being subordinate to men, and the positive value of living apart from the world. In these beliefs, he had chosen a simple orphan girl, Sabrina, and attempted to raise her in seclusion to one day be his wife, educating her only in those skills he deemed necessary for his happiness. The experiment failed, but Maria must have been aware of it, as she later used the idea in the plot of her first society novel, *Belinda*.

Day first realised the inadequacies of his bride-to-be when in 1771, he became acquainted with Honora Sneyd, two years before she became Maria's stepmother. Convinced of Honora's superiority to Sabrina, Day sought Honora's hand in marriage. In his proposal letter, he wrote of his intention to live a secluded life and presented his views on the superiority of men. Honora refused him, reasoning that the best foundation for a happy marriage was 'terms of reasonable equality'[2] between husband and wife. She categorically refused to submit to 'the unqualified control of a husband over all her actions'[2] or to live in seclusion.

Letters for Literary Ladies takes the form of two letters. The opinions expressed in this fictional exchange of letters reflected Day's position and Maria's response. The first character advises against educating women beyond a certain point because it makes them unmarriageable, whereas Maria's views are clearly expressed in the response, emphasising that clever men like wives with whom they can have intelligent conversation. These views were clearly imbued in Maria as a young girl by her stepmother, Honora, and confirmed through observation. It is hard to judge how much Maria knew of her own mother's inadequacies as an intelligent companion as she died when Maria was only 5, but she was witness of the felicity in marriage enjoyed by her father and his later wives.

Letters for Literary Ladies was published in the same volume as *Letters of Julia and Caroline* – a series of letters designed to encourage young ladies to choose their marriage partners wisely, by means of a cautionary tale – and an *Essay on the Noble Science of Self-justification*. The latter advised the reader how to justify themselves in such a sarcastic tone that the advice was clearly not meant to be followed.

In 1797 Maria had to console yet more of her half-siblings when their mother, Elizabeth, died. In keeping with what was becoming a tradition, her father soon married again. This time he chose Frances Beaufort, a vicar's daughter who was a year younger than Maria. This may have been expected to cause resentment, but there is no suggestion that Maria objected to the age of her new stepmother. Frances had drawn some of the illustrations in Maria's work and the two women became good friends. Maria never married, living in her father's house until his death, and afterwards, with Frances, for the rest of her life.

A narrow escape from death
Life in Ireland was not without its excitement. In 1798, the Irish rebelled against British rule. In June, Maria wrote to her cousin: 'All has been quiet in our county, and we know nothing of the dreadful disturbances in other parts of the country but what we see in the newspapers.'[3] But this peace was soon broken. Two years earlier, in 1796, the French had attempted to invade Ireland in support of the rebels, but had been thwarted by bad

weather. They tried again in August 1798 and landed successfully in the west and reached Castlebar, about eighty miles from Edgeworthstown.

That August, Maria wrote of their frustration in not knowing what was happening. 'We who are so near the scene of action cannot by any means discover what number of the French actually landed: some say 800, some 1,800, some 18,000, some 4,000.'[4] The actual figure was around 1,000, however they were joined by greater numbers of Irish rebels and enjoyed some initial successes.

As reports came in that the rebels were within a few miles of Edgeworthstown, Maria and her family prepared to leave their home. A small group of British soldiers escorting an ammunition cart to Longford promised to conduct them to safety. For some reason, Maria's father detained the family and so the soldiers left without them. Maria wrote:

Half an hour afterwards, as we were quietly sitting in the portico, we heard—as we thought close to us—a clap of thunder, which shook the house. The officer soon afterwards returned, almost speechless; he could hardly explain what had happened. The ammunition cart, containing nearly three barrels of gunpowder, packed in tin cases, took fire and burst, halfway on the road to Longford. She concluded: *If we had gone with this ammunition, we must have been killed.*[5]

A few hours later, Maria fled to a nearby inn with her family as 300 pikemen were within a mile of Edgeworthstown. On 8 September, the main rebel force was decisively defeated at the Battle of Ballinamuck, just fifteen miles north of Edgeworthstown.

The day after the battle, Maria returned home, 'where everything was exactly as we had left it, all serene and happy, five days before – only five days, which seemed almost a lifetime, from the dangers and anxiety we had gone through'.[6]

Practical Education
Against this background of military activity and civil unrest, Maria and her father published the book that accelerated her journey to becoming a household name. Despite their passion for storytelling, this was not fiction, but a manual on the education of children, entitled *Practical Education*.

This father-daughter collaboration was rooted in their experimental methods of teaching the younger Edgeworth children.

The book examined various areas of a child's upbringing. It provided advice about toys, advocated the complete separation of children from servants, and looked at subject areas from mathematics and mechanics, to geography and literature, providing ideas as to how these subjects could be taught in order to engage the pupils' interest. Moreover, the publication gave advice for forming character with sections on honesty, taste, and economy, and contained practical ideas to stimulate learning, such as a globe of silk painted with the countries of the world on it, and lists of experiments.

The British Critic and Quarterly Theological Review slated *Practical Education*:

> *Here, readers, is education a-la-mode, in the true style of modern Philosophy; nearly 800 quarto pages on practical Education, and not a word on God, Religion, Christianity, or a hint that such topics are ever to be mentioned.* It concluded: *The rambling, flimsy manner in which these volumes are written, is well worthy of the system they are intended to support; but we are willing to hope that few English parents are far enough advanced in Philosophy, to wish to give their children the advantages of such an education.*[7]

Despite such negative reviews, *Practical Education* proved popular and led to a degree of recognition for its two authors. Maria loved working with her father and called their literary partnership 'the joy and pride of my life'.[8]

Castle Rackrent

But it was Maria's novels that made her famous in her lifetime, particularly her first, *Castle Rackrent*. Published in 1800, *Castle Rackrent* told the story of several generations of fictional Irish landowners. It combined Maria's love of storytelling with her enthusiasm for education: she sought to teach about the past through fiction rather than biography or history. The action takes place in Ireland in the years running up to 1782. It was intended as a historical rather than a contemporary perspective on Irish landowners and their behaviour – an insight into the Irish people of the near past, but nevertheless, historical.

The book was a huge success and entered its second edition before the year was out. As was common at the time, particularly for women writers, the book was published anonymously. Such was its popularity that another writer tried to claim it as their own and went so far as to forge pages of what they claimed to be the original manuscript! The third edition appeared in 1801, this time with Maria's name on the cover.

Much of the detail of the novel was based on Maria's own experience. The Edgeworth family had been landowners for generations and Maria was only too aware of how the family estate had been neglected before her family removed to Ireland in 1782. Maria's experience as rent collector and accountant for her father enabled her to add genuine details to the story. The narrator of *Castle Rackrent*, Honest Thady, was based on an Irish agent that Maria had met when she had first come to Ireland, and whose character struck her so much that the story grew up around him.

It was the first novel in English about Ireland – what some call a regional novel – and sought to bring to life the customs of the Irish people in a favourable light. It used Irish dialect and usefully included a glossary explaining some of the more unusual terms to make it more accessible to an English readership. This was particularly poignant because of the time it was published – the eve of the union with Great Britain, which came into force on 1 January 1801. It has been said that Maria Edgeworth's *Castle Rackrent* did more for easing the union of Ireland with the rest of the United Kingdom than any other policy or work.

Being a novel, *Castle Rackrent* was not taken as seriously at the time as a history or other non-fiction work. A few reviews appeared, which were generally favourable. *The British Critic* said: 'This is a very pleasant, good-humoured, and successful representation of the eccentricities of our Irish neighbours.'[9]

Perhaps Maria Edgeworth's biggest fan was Sir Walter Scott. In a foreword to his first *Waverley* novel, he acknowledged the debt he owed Maria. Her success in painting a picture of the Irish people prompted him to complete a work that would do the same for the Scottish. Today, it is Scott's *Waverley* novels that remain famous; *Castle Rackrent* is virtually forgotten. And yet without *Castle Rackrent*, would *Waverley* ever have made it to the publishers?

Maria's first novel was also her most successful. The notes to the 1903 edition of *Castle Rackrent* claimed: 'The little volume contains the history of a nation. It is a masterpiece which Miss Edgeworth has never surpassed.'[10]

The Concise Oxford Companion to English Literature said of *Castle Rackrent*: 'This work may be regarded as the first fully developed historical novel and the first true regional novel in English'.[11] It was also the first novel to centre the story on a 'big house', and over several generations – what is now referred to as a saga novel. Maria wrote other works about Ireland including *The Absentee* and *Ennui*, but none were as successful as her first.

Belinda and other novels

Maria's second novel, *Belinda*, published in 1801, was completely different from *Castle Rackrent*. *Belinda* was a society novel and, like many of her subsequent books, it was centred on the female characters and intended to be an instructive, moral tale. In *Belinda*, she looked at the serious subjects of nationality and gender and the dangers of gambling.

In the foreword, Maria specifically distanced herself from the popular novel of the day:

> *The following work is offered to the public as a Moral Tale – the author not wishing to acknowledge a Novel. Were all novels like those of Madame de Crousaz, Mrs Inchbald, Miss Burney, or Dr Moore, she would adopt the name of novel with delight: But so much folly, errour, and vice are disseminated in the books classed under this denomination, that it is hoped the wish to assume another title will be attributed to feelings that are laudable, and not fastidious.*[12]

Belinda was well received and as early as 1802, it was translated into French. Her other fictional writings were mostly reviewed favourably and her second series of *Tales of Fashionable Life* earned her £1,050 making her more financially successful as a novelist than any of her contemporaries. Maria published her last full length novel, *Helen*, in 1834.

Maria later wrote about the way in which she created her characters:

> *I have seldom or ever drawn any one character – certainly not any*

ridiculous or faulty character, from any individual. Wherever, in writing, a real character rose to my view, from memory or resemblance, it has always been hurtful to me, because, to avoid that resemblance, I was tempted by cowardice or compelled by conscience to throw in differences, which often ended in making my character inconsistent, unreal.[13]

A marriage proposal

In 1802, during the Peace of Amiens, Maria travelled to Europe in the company of her father. They were well-received on account of the success of *Practical Education*. Maria's half-brother Lovell was less fortunate. He was imprisoned in France when the peace collapsed and was not freed until Napoleon's forces were defeated in 1814.

It was at this time that Maria received her only known proposal of marriage. Her suitor was a Swedish courtier called Abraham Niclas Clewberg-Edelcrantz. He was a clever man who shared her father's scientific interests and there is no doubt that Maria was very fond of him and enjoyed being in his company. Maria described Edelcrantz in a letter to her aunt as 'a Swedish gentleman, whom we have mentioned to you, of superior understanding and mild manners: he came to offer me his hand and heart!!'[14]

Maria was steadfast in her refusal. Her stepmother later wrote that she thought Maria was more in love than she realised at the time. So why, if Maria was in love, did she refuse Monsieur Edelcrantz? The trouble was his sense of duty. He considered himself, first and foremost, to be committed to his position at court and therefore required Maria, if she became his wife, to live in Sweden with him. However much in love with him she was, Maria realised what it would mean to her family if she married him and, most particularly, what it would do to her father if she left never to return. Despite his early neglect of her, Maria was devoted to her father's interests. It seemed that not even a lover could surpass him in her affections and so she refused the only marriage proposal that we know she received.

Perhaps she never recovered from his lost love. After her refusal, there was a loss of friendship which she felt keenly. She wrote *Leonora* – a romantic novel in letter-form. It was a style that she knew Edelcrantz would like, but she never discovered whether he ever read it. Even after the Swedish king abdicated, Edelcrantz remained in Sweden and never sought Maria's hand again. His pride would not let him chase after her having been rejected, but it seems that he never forgot her, remaining unmarried until his death.

Regency celebrity

Although Edgeworthstown remained Maria's home, she often went visiting, touring Ireland and Scotland, and staying in London. Her celebrity status brought her into contact with all kinds of famous people and she shared her thoughts about them in the many letters she wrote to her friends and relations.

Visiting London in 1813, she was not impressed by the poet Lord Byron, writing disparagingly: 'His appearance is nothing that you would remark.'[15] The political economist, David Ricardo, made a better impression: 'He is altogether one of the most agreeable persons, as well as the best informed and most clever, that I ever knew.'[16]

She was able to rekindle her friendship with Kitty Pakenham, who was now married to the Duke of Wellington:

Charming, amiable Lady Wellington! As she truly said of herself, she is always 'Kitty Pakenham to her friends'. After comparison with crowds of others, beaux esprits, fine ladies and fashionable scramblers for notoriety, her dignified graceful simplicity rises in one's opinion, and we feel it with more conviction of its superiority.[17]

Although Maria was 'gratified by her "success" in the society of her celebrated contemporaries, she never varied in her love for Home'.[18]

She loved to read and was familiar with the works of her contemporaries including Fanny Burney and Jane Austen. She wrote of Fanny Burney's novel *Cecilia*: 'Charlotte cordials me twice a day with *Cecilia*, which she reads charmingly, and which entertains me as much at the third reading as it did at the first.'[19] She wrote of Jane Austen's writing: 'We have been much entertained with *Mansfield Park*.'[20]

Maria was very well organised, as her first stepmother Honora had taught her, and managed to get through a lot of work every day. She was at ease in the busy Edgeworth household and did not shut herself away to work, but usually wrote in the library, undisturbed by the noise of the large family about her.

In 1817, Maria lost the single most influential person in her life with the death of her father. Maria had the greatest respect for his abilities and had always been subservient to his opinion, allowing him to edit her work throughout his life. Whilst there is no doubt that he encouraged her development as a writer, submitting to his judgement did not always alter her writing for the better.

Grief, perhaps combined with overwork, brought on a recurrence of the eye problems that Maria had endured years before. She stayed several months with her aunt at Black Castle, resting her eyes, neither writing nor reading more than absolutely necessary. For nearly two years, she rested her weak eyes as much as possible. She wrote very few letters, though she still struggled to complete her father's memoirs, as he had requested. By the autumn of 1819, her eyes were better and she exulted in having 'a little time, and eyes to read again', claiming a 'voracious appetite' for reading matter 'good, bad, and indifferent'.[21] But the rest had paid off. She never struggled with her eyes again. Her father's memoirs were finally published in 1820, but they were not very well received and the *Quarterly Review* was far from complimentary.

In London, Maria met the great abolitionist William Wilberforce many times. 'He is very lively, and full of odd contortions: no matter. His indulgent, benevolent temper strikes me particularly: he makes no pretension to superior sanctity or strictness.'[22] She was opposed to the slave trade and wrote: 'We went on board a slave-ship with my brother, and saw the dreadfully small hole in which the poor slaves are stowed together, so that they cannot stir.'[23] Maria went about in society, visiting Almack's Assembly Rooms and socialising with people of fashion and learning, such as fellow educational writer Jane Marcet. She saw prison reformer Elizabeth Fry at work in Newgate Prison, and met actress Sarah Siddons whom she found 'exceedingly entertaining, told anecdotes, repeated some passages from *Jane Shore* beautifully, and invited us to a private evening party at her house.'[24]

After reading *Waverley*, Maria began a correspondence with Sir Walter Scott and developed a strong friendship with him and his family, visiting him at his Abbotsford home in 1823. He in turn visited Edgeworthstown in 1825. Maria wrote of her first impression of Sir Walter:

His countenance, even by the uncertain light in which I first saw it, pleased me much, benevolent, and full of genius without the slightest effort at expression; delightfully natural, as if he did not know he was Walter Scott or the Great Unknown of the North, as if he only thought of making others happy.[25]

After her father's death, Maria continued to live at Edgeworthstown, which was now owned by her half-brother Lovell Edgeworth. Initially she gave up the management of the estate, but in 1826, she was persuaded to take control again to help her brother through a major financial crisis. By means of careful money management, Maria enabled her brother to survive without selling off his land.

What was Maria like?
American George Ticknor, Professor of Modern Literature at Harvard University, visited Edgeworthstown in 1835. He described Maria as:

A small, short, spare lady of about sixty-seven, with extremely frank and kind manners, and who always looks straight into your face with a pair of mild deep gray eyes whenever she speaks to you. Her conversation, always ready, is as full of vivacity and variety as I can imagine. It is also no less full of good-nature. She is disposed to defend everybody, as far as she can, though never so far as to be unreasonable.[26]

Her stepmother Frances Edgeworth said of her: 'No one ever conversed with her for five minutes without forgetting the plainness of her features in the vivacity, benevolence, and genius expressed in her countenance.'[27]

English writer and clergyman Sydney Smith was enchanted with Maria. He wrote: 'Miss Edgeworth was delightful, so clever and sensible. She does not say witty things, but there is such a perfume of wit runs through all her conversation as makes it very brilliant.'[28]

Last years
In the 1830s, Sir William Rowan Hamilton, president of the Royal Irish Academy, asked Maria's advice on how to advance the spread of polite literature in Ireland. She replied at length and included in her recommendations admitting women to the Academy's evening parties. Maria was the second woman to be elected an honorary member of the Royal Irish Academy in 1842.

Maria maintained a love of reading to the very end of her life. 'Our pleasures in literature do not, I think, decline with age; last 1st of January was my eighty-second birthday, and I think that I had as much enjoyment from books as I ever had in my life.'[1] [29]

Maria died on 22 May 1849 in Edgeworthstown, where she was buried in St John's churchyard. She was 81 years old and not 82 as suggested by the quote above, where she seems to have misremembered her own age.

Maria's legacy
Maria Edgeworth was the most commercially successful novelist of her time and yet her works are largely unknown today. She was a strong advocate for the education of women, but her *Practical Education* has long since been forgotten. Yet Maria Edgeworth started a genre of book that we take for granted today – the genre of historical fiction. What she began, others have taken up.

Chapter 7

Faraday's Teacher – Jane Marcet (1769–1858)

At the end of the eighteenth century, it was fashionable to take an interest in science. The Royal Institution was founded in 1799 to encourage continual scientific development and its applications into agriculture and industry. Its lectures were designed to introduce new technologies and teach science to the general public. Both men and women could attend these lectures, but there was a world of difference between being allowed to attend and understanding what was being said. Without being educated in scientific language, as most women weren't, the lectures were virtually impossible to understand. What was needed was a '*Dummies* guide' to bridge the gap.

Jane Marcet wrote that guide. Her book, *Conversations on Chemistry*, was written with the express aim of making the Royal Institution lectures understandable. It was written by a woman for women, but it was not just women who benefited. It helped a blacksmith's son, Michael Faraday, grasp the basic principles of chemistry and inspired him to take up a career in science which led to some of the greatest scientific discoveries ever made – discoveries that have shaped our modern world.

Early life
Jane was fortunate to be raised in a home where all the children, not just the boys, were taught Latin and science. She was the eldest of the twelve children of Anthony Francis Haldimand, a naturalised Englishman from a family of wealthy Swiss merchants, and Jane Pickersgill, a London merchant's daughter. Jane was born in London where she was baptised on 23 June 1769. Her father's business was based in St Mary Axe – the area of London which today boasts the landmark building of 20 St Mary Axe, better known as The Gherkin.

Jane's childhood came to an abrupt end in 1785, when her mother died, shortly after giving birth to her youngest son. The 16-year-old Jane took over the management of her father's household and helped to bring up her younger siblings. She also became her father's close companion, acting as hostess when he entertained some of the most eminent scientific and literary characters of the day. In the late 1780s, Jane accompanied her father on a trip to Italy sparking an interest in art, which she followed up with lessons from Sir Joshua Reynolds and Sir Thomas Lawrence. She later employed her artistic skill to illustrate her own books.

In 1791, Jane's father inherited the estate and business of his uncle, Sir Frederick Haldimand – a fortune that Jane later benefited from.

A scientific husband
Bringing up a bevy of younger siblings did not make Jane's situation conducive to an early marriage. At the age of 30, she was still single and perhaps she would have remained that way if it wasn't for one of her father's scientific visitors – a Genevan-born doctor named Alexander Marcet.

Alexander John Gaspard Marcet was from a family of wealthy Swiss merchants, but rather than follow his father into trade, he wanted to study science. During the unrest in Geneva in the wake of the French Revolution, he was imprisoned for having once served in the National Guard. Fortunately, rather than going to the guillotine, his sentence was commuted to five years' exile and in 1794, he went to Edinburgh to study medicine, accompanied by his close friend, Charles Gaspard De la Rive. After qualifying as a doctor, he moved to London and was appointed physician to the City Dispensary at Finsbury. Alexander and Jane were married in Battersea on 4 December 1799. It was a happy marriage but Jane seems to have suffered from some kind of depression – possibly post-natal depression after the birth of their first child, Francis, in 1803. Alexander's career went from strength to strength. In 1804, he was appointed a physician at Guy's Hospital and the following year, he co-founded the Medico-Chirurgical Society. But Alexander's real passion was chemistry. He took every opportunity to deepen his knowledge of the subject and created his own laboratory so that he could perform practical experiments. He conducted experimental analysis of mineral water and sea water and started to prepare a course of lectures on basic chemistry.

Jane was eager to share in her husband's passion for chemistry and, like many of her contemporaries, she attended Humphry Davy's lectures at the Royal Institution in Albemarle Street, London. Humphry Davy was the Director of the Laboratory at the Royal Institution and he gave his first Royal Institution lecture to the public in 1801. Davy was a Cornish chemist who had established himself as a leading scientist through his research on gases, in particular, his discovery of the properties of nitrous oxide – laughing gas. He went on to isolate various chemical elements including potassium, sodium and calcium, but he is perhaps most remembered for the Davy lamp – a safety lamp that was of great value to the mining community. Davy helped establish the Royal Institution's reputation as a popular venue for brilliant scientific lectures.

Jane had a basic grounding in science from the education she had received at home which had also equipped her with a knowledge of Latin – absolutely essential for a study of the sciences at the time. But even with this knowledge, she found that the lectures went too fast for her to comprehend and she came out confused and full of questions. Fortunately, she was able to talk through the concepts with her husband, who understood her need to learn and helped her to grasp a better understanding of what she had heard.

Conversations on Chemistry

Jane soon realised that she was not the only person to come away from Davy's lectures with more questions than answers. Very few of the women who attended these lectures had her advantages – a basic knowledge of science and Latin and their own private tutor. She decided to develop a resource that would help ordinary people, particularly women, to grasp the substance of what she had delighted in learning. And so her 'Conversations on …' series was born, starting with Conversations on Chemistry – the Georgian equivalent to a 'Dummies guide' to chemistry.

Years before, while she was helping to bring up her younger siblings, Jane had developed a short course on natural philosophy – what we would call physics – in the form of natural dialogues between three characters: Mrs B, the teacher, and her two pupils – the studious Emily and the cheerfully casual Caroline.

Jane must have found this technique successful as she remembered the format she had used and thought the same approach might work for a basic course in chemistry. Encouraged by her husband, she started to develop a series of conversations around the subject. Although she had already written some conversations on natural philosophy, she decided not to publish them at this time because there was already a work entitled *Scientific Dialogues*, which covered similar ground. Jane used the same three characters – Mrs B, Emily and Caroline – to write her *Conversations on Chemistry*. Using conversation as a means of teaching was not a new idea, but Jane was the first person to use exclusively female characters. As Mrs B taught, her pupils asked questions that she then attempted to answer, or they made observations, which she sought to correct or amplify.

This is an excerpt from the first conversation – *On the general principles of chemistry* – in which Mrs B attempts to explain the difference between decomposition and division:

EMILY
I thought that decomposing a body was dividing it into its minutest parts. And if so, I do not understand why an elementary substance is not capable of being decomposed, as well as any other.
MRS B
You have misconceived the idea of decomposition; it is very different from mere division. The latter simply reduces a body into parts, but the former separates it into the various ingredients, or materials, of which it is composed. If we were to take a loaf of bread, and separate the several ingredients of which it is made, the flour, the yeast, the salt, and the water, it would be very different from cutting or crumbling the loaf into pieces.
EMILY
I understand you now very well. To decompose a body is to separate from each other the various elementary substances of which it consists.
CAROLINE
But flour, water, and other materials of bread, according to our definition, are not elementary substances?
MRS B
No, my dear; I mentioned bread rather as a familiar comparison, to illustrate the idea, than as an example. The elementary substances of which a body is composed are called the constituent parts of that body; in decomposing it, therefore, we separate its constituent parts. If, on the contrary, we divide a body by chopping

it to pieces, or even by grinding or pounding it to the finest powder,
each of these small particles will still consist of a portion of the
several constituent parts of the whole body: these are called the
integrant parts; do you understand the difference?
EMILY
Yes, I think, perfectly. We decompose a body into its constituent
parts; and divide it into its integrant parts.[1]

For the time, this was considered relatively informal and easy to
understand. What made Jane's work so accessible was that she used
everyday objects, such as bread in the above example, to illustrate
scientific concepts. There was no need of Latin or even any previous
scientific understanding to be able to grasp what she was saying. She gave
people the tools to help them understand Davy's lectures, not by
eliminating the technical language, but by explaining what it meant.

By means of practical experiments and the process of question and
answer, the pupils, and hence the reader, learned about chemistry. The
book included a number of illustrations drawn by Jane herself. Most were
original, depicting experiments Alexander had set up for her, although a
few were copies of engravings from other scientific works.

Conversations encouraged its readers to try the experiments for
themselves. They were depicted as having been performed by Mrs B and
her pupils, thereby conveying the notion that they were perfectly suitable
for women to attempt. The experiments ranged from the very simple, such
as adding water to quicklime, to the quite complicated and even
potentially dangerous.

Alexander was always on hand to correct Jane's work when she got
something wrong and he made suggestions on points of style. Working
so closely together caused some tension in their marriage, and
occasionally they regretted having ever started the project. However,
Alexander recorded in his journal that the 'exchange of thinking' was
useful to them both and he believed that the benefits of this would outlast
the memory of the quarrels that the collaboration had caused.[2]

A humble approach
Jane approached the whole project with considerable diffidence. She felt
that she was a relative novice and hesitated to publish a work that some
might think presumptuous. Perhaps because of this innate modesty, or

perhaps a fear that the book's inadequacies might reflect badly on her husband, *Conversations on Chemistry* was published anonymously in 1805.

The introduction to the book made it clear that it was written by a female author, and a modest one at that.

> *In venturing to offer to the public, and more particularly to the female sex, an Introduction to Chemistry, the author, herself a woman, conceives that some explanation may be required; and she feels it the more necessary to apologise for the present undertaking, as her knowledge of the subject is but recent, and as she can have no real claims to the title of chemist.*[3]

The scientific circle in which the Marcets moved provided plenty of opportunity for feedback on her work. Jane showed her dialogues to the prominent Genevan scientific journalist Marc-Auguste Pictet who was visiting the Marcets at the time. He was impressed with what he saw and encouraged her to persevere. Another of Alexander's associates, Dr Yelloly, the English physician with whom Alexander founded the Royal Medical and Chirurgical Society, was asked for his opinion, which was also favourable. He made some suggestions for improving the text, largely concerned with matters of style. Jane's approach was a little too familiar for these academics and she was urged to make her style less chatty. This is perhaps surprising considering the complexity of some of the language and sentence structure used in the text! Yelloly negotiated a favourable publishing deal with Longman for Jane's book. Longman arranged for yet another male academic to check over the script – this time Arthur Aikin, an English chemist and scientific writer. When he gave it his seal of approval, Longman offered to publish Jane's *Conversations on Chemistry* at no cost to the Marcets, taking instead a share of the profits as their payment.

Conversations on Chemistry was a huge success and was regularly updated, running to sixteen editions in England. According to Longman's records, *Conversations on Chemistry* had sold 20,000 copies by 1865. It wasn't until the twelfth edition in 1832 that Jane's name appeared on the cover for the first time.

It was also extremely popular in America, where it is estimated that around 160,000 copies were sold, including one to US President Thomas

Jefferson. The American version went through twenty-three editions plus a further twelve editions of an unauthorised adaptation by Thomas Jones called *New Conversations on Chemistry*. There was nothing Jane could do about her work being copied as US copyright laws did not extend to foreign publications, meaning that American publishers could revise, alter and extend her work as much as they liked.

Conversations on Chemistry proved very popular as a textbook for teaching chemistry to girls in American schools. In the introduction of his unauthorised adaptation in 1832, Jones wrote: 'The *Conversations on Chemistry*, written by Mrs Marcet, have acquired and sustained a deservedly high reputation, and have undoubtedly contributed more than any other work to promote the study of chemistry as a popular branch of education.'[4] Jane's work was translated into other languages, including French and German, and sold in continental Europe.

Faraday's first instructress
With her *Conversations on Chemistry*, Jane succeeded in making science accessible to the ordinary people of her day who had not had the advantage of much education. One of these was Michael Faraday.

Faraday was the son of a blacksmith with little formal schooling and yet he became one of the most famous English scientists, undertaking extensive research into electromagnetism and electrochemistry. The development of his ideas allowed electricity to be turned into a useful power source. He also made advances in chemistry, discovering benzene, liquefying chlorine and inventing an early form of Bunsen burner.

Perhaps encouraged by his own recollections of his limited knowledge when he started his scientific career, Faraday founded two series of introductory lectures at the Royal Institution: the Christmas lectures designed for children, and the Friday evening discourses designed for non-scientists. He became the first Fullerian Professor of Chemistry at the Royal Institution. He gave his name to the unit of capacitance, the Farad, and gave expert advice to institutions such as the National Gallery and the British Museum about conservation.

After Jane's death, Faraday was asked if it was true that he had, indeed, been inspired by Jane's writing. Faraday replied that he had been working for a bookseller and bookbinder since the age of 13. His employer had encouraged him to read the books that he was working on and he had delighted in the books on science.

There were two that especially helped me, the Encyclopaedia Britannica, *from which I gained my first notions of electricity, and Mrs Marcet's* Conversations on Chemistry, *which gave me my foundation in that science. Do not suppose that I was a very deep thinker, or was marked as a precocious person. I was a very lively, imaginative person, and could believe in the* Arabian Nights *as easily as in the* Encyclopaedia; *but facts were important to me, and saved me. I could trust a fact, and always cross-examined an assertion. So when I questioned Mrs Marcet's book by such little experiments as I could find means to perform, and found it true to the facts as I could understand them, I felt that I had got hold of an anchor in chemical knowledge, and clung fast to it. Thence my deep veneration for Mrs Marcet: first, as one who had conferred great personal good and pleasure on me, and then as one able to convey the truth and principle of those boundless fields of knowledge which concern natural things, to the young, untaught, and inquiring mind.*[5]

In later years, Faraday was delighted to become personally acquainted with Jane, whom he described as his 'first instructress'.[6] It is fascinating to observe that the process went full circle and Faraday's discoveries became new source material for later editions of Jane's *Conversations on Chemistry*.

Family life takes over
Despite the success of her *Conversations on Chemistry*, Jane did not immediately start work on another book. For a while at least, her time was taken up with family matters, with the birth of her daughter Louisa in 1807. In the same year, Alexander started lecturing on chemistry at Guy's Hospital, something he continued until 1820. He accompanied his lectures with practical demonstrations, which was quite unusual for the time. In 1808, Alexander was made a fellow of the Royal Society. Jane gave birth to a second daughter, Sophia, in 1809. It must have been hard for her when Alexander went off to Portsmouth where he had volunteered to manage the temporary military hospital to look after the fever-stricken soldiers returning from the disastrous Walcheren campaign. Even worse, Alexander caught the fever and was very ill for a time. At the Congress of Vienna, Alexander's home town of Geneva was restored to

independence and he took advantage of this new-found freedom to take his family on a visit there in 1815.

Conversations on Political Economy

When Jane turned her mind to writing again, she took up the subject of economics. Abandoning the studious Emily and using just two characters, Mrs B and the outspoken Caroline, she introduced the basic concepts of economics in another book: *Conversations on Political Economy*. It was published 'by the author of *Conversations on Chemistry*' in 1816.[7]

Just as *Conversations on Chemistry* was the product of her own learning, so too was *Conversations on Political Economy*. Jane moved in the same intellectual circles as the leading political economists and spent a lot of time listening to what was being said. By creating a dialogue about the topics being discussed, she was able to clarify her own ideas. In the introduction, Jane wrote that it was an attempt

> . . . *to bring within the reach of young persons a science which no English writer has yet presented in an easy and familiar form.*[8]

She went on to say that:

> *Political Economy, though so immediately connected with the happiness and improvement of mankind, and the object of so much controversy and speculation among men of knowledge, is not yet become a popular science, and is not generally considered as a study essential to early education.*[8]

Jane's *Conversations on Political Economy* changed this. In 1822, Maria Edgeworth wrote: 'Fine ladies require that their daughters' governesses should teach Political Economy. "Do you teach Political Economy?" "No, but I can learn it." "O dear, no; if you don't teach it, you won't do for me."'[9] Jane's *Conversations on Political Economy* must, in some measure, be responsible for this change in attitude.

Jane openly admitted in her preface that her work contained no original ideas, but was based on the works of the great classical economists of her day – Adam Smith, Thomas Malthus, Jean-Baptiste Say and Jean Charles Léonard de Sismondi. She also drew on the economics of David Ricardo, a great advocate of free trade, whose most important work, *Principles of*

Political Economy and Taxation, was published the year after Jane's *Conversations on Political Economy*.

As Jane was friends with many of the leading economists, including Malthus and Ricardo, it is likely she was referring to them in the preface as those from whom she 'derived great assistance' and who 'revised her sheets as she advanced in the undertaking'.[10]

In the introduction to *Conversations on Political Economy*, Jane explained why she believed it was important to study it:

> *CAROLINE*
> *Well, after all, Mrs B, ignorance of political economy is a very excusable deficiency in women. It is the business of Government to reform the prejudices and errors which prevail respecting it; and as we are never likely to become legislators, is it not just as well that we should remain in happy ignorance of evils which we have no power to remedy?*
> *MRS B*
> *When you plead in favour of ignorance, there is a strong presumption that you are in the wrong. If a more general knowledge of political economy prevented women from propagating errors respecting it, no trifling good would ensue. Childhood is spent in acquiring ideas, adolescence in discriminating and rejecting those which are false; how greatly we should facilitate this labour by diminishing the number of errors imbided in early youth, and by inculcating such ideas only as are founded in truth.*
> *CAROLINE*
> *Surely you would not teach political economy to children?*
> *MRS B*
> *I would wish that mothers were so far competent to teach it, that their children should not have anything to unlearn.*[11]

Jane's *Conversations on Political Economy* inspired essayist and journalist Harriet Martineau to bring economic matters into her work. Harriet Martineau wrote:

> *She administered to young minds large supplies of the wisdom of Adam Smith, in a form almost as entertaining as the 'Wealth of Nations' is to grown readers. Her intimate acquaintance with Say,*

100

King's Statue, Weymouth – a
Coade stone statue of George III.

The entrance to
Coade and Sealy's
artificial stone gallery.

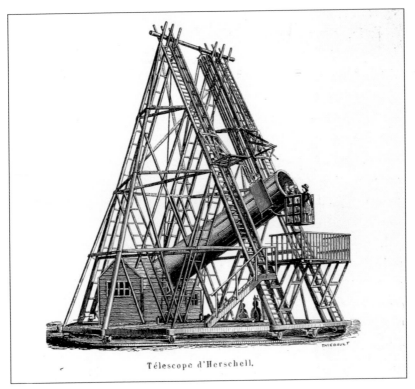

Télescope d'Herschell.

William Herschel's telescope.

Drury Lane Theatre from the stage during a performance.

Mrs Siddons as the Tragic Muse by Sir Joshua Reynolds.

Madame Tussaud.

A la Ronde. With kind permission of
the National Trust.

Maria Edgeworth.

The Royal Institution, Albemarle
Street, London.

An illustration from
Conversations on Chemistry
by Jane Marcet.

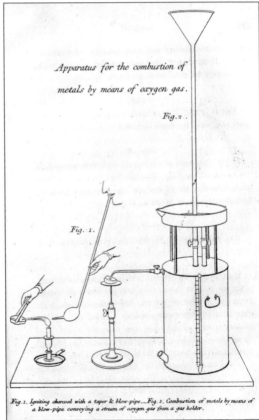

*Apparatus for the combustion of
metals by means of oxygen gas.*

Fig. 2.

Fig. 1.

Fig. 1. Igniting charcoal with a taper & blow-pipe.—Fig. 2. Combustion of metals by means of
a blow-pipe conveying a stream of oxygen gas from a gas holder.

Clifton Suspension Bridge.

Chawton Cottage, now Jane Austen's House Museum, Hampshire.

Jane Austen Festival 2014 Regency Promenade in Bath.

Harriot Coutts (née Mellon).

Elizabeth Fry visits Newgate Prison.

Fossils on the beach at Lyme Regis, Dorset.

Malthus, and other chiefs of that department of knowledge, helped
to enrich her work with some modern developments.[12]

Her natural diffidence continued. In 1822, Maria Edgeworth observed:
'It has now become high fashion with blue ladies to talk Political
Economy, and make a great jabbering on the subject, while others who
have more sense, like Mrs Marcet, hold their tongues and listen.'[9] This is
a fascinating observation on Jane's quiet character, for by this time,
Conversations on Political Economy had been out for some years and
presumably Jane knew as much about the subject as any of her female
contemporaries!

Martineau also credited Jane with having had 'unquestionably some
share' in bringing on 'the irreversible establishment of Free Trade in
England' which was 'a blessing which she deserved to witness.'[13]

Though not as successful as *Conversations on Chemistry*,
Conversations on Political Economy still went through seven editions and
was gratefully received by those looking for a simple approach to a
subject that many people found overwhelmingly complicated.

The impact of an inheritance
In 1817, Jane's father died. His fortune was divided between his four
surviving children, including Jane and her brother William – a director
of the Bank of England – and their cousins. The inheritance that the
Marcets received allowed Alexander to resign his post at Guy's Hospital
and concentrate his energies on chemical research. He published *An Essay
on the Chemical History and Medical Treatment of Calculous Disorders*,
the results of his most important research, in the same year.

With the success of her first two books, Jane was encouraged to revise
and publish the script for her original book of conversations on physics.
Conversations on Natural Philosophy was published in 1819 running to
at least thirteen editions.

In 1820, Alexander stopped lecturing at Guy's Hospital and was free
to take his family on an extended visit to Geneva. Whilst there, they were
visited by Maria Edgeworth whom they had become friends with in
London. Edgeworth wrote:

We came here last Friday, and have spent our time most happily
with our excellent friend Mrs Marcet. His children are all so fond

of Dr Marcet, we see that he is their companion and friend. They have all been happily busy in making a paper fire-balloon, sixteen feet in diameter, and thirty feet high. A large company were invited to see it mount. It was a fine evening. The balloon was filled on the green before the house. The lawn slopes down to the lake, and opposite to it magnificent Mont Blanc, the setting sun shining on its summit. After some heartbeatings about a hole in the top of the balloon, through which the smoke was seen to issue—an evil omen—it went up successfully. The sun had set, but we saw its reflection beautifully on one side of the balloon, so that it looked like a globe half ice, half fire, or half moon, half sun, self-suspended in the air. It went up exactly a mile.[14]

Whilst in Geneva, Alexander was appointed Honorary Professor of Chemistry at the university and he gave a course of lectures there in the spring of 1820. The warmth of the scientific community in Geneva persuaded Alexander to settle his family permanently in Switzerland. But things didn't work out as he had planned. In 1822, the family returned to England to prepare for their permanent removal. Alexander visited Edinburgh before returning to London, and became ill very suddenly with a 'gout in the stomach'.[15] Though attended by some of the most eminent physicians of the day, Alexander died in London on 19 October.

Later writings
After Alexander's death, Jane continued to update her earlier books and added two new titles to her *Conversations* series. She wrote *Conversations on the Evidences of Christianity*, published in 1826, 'to recommend Christianity, as defended in the pages of its best advocates.'[16] Interestingly, in this volume she moved away from her usual characters and had Mr B in conversation with two different children, Beatrice and Edward. Perhaps when it came to religion she felt that a male teacher carried more authority.

In *Conversations on Vegetable Physiology*, published in 1829, Jane reverted to her previous characters, Mrs B, Emily and Caroline. These *Conversations* were based on the work of her friend the Swiss botanist, Augustin Pyramus de Candolle. It was not as successful as her early books and only went into three editions. Jane also wrote another book on economics, *John Hopkins's Notions on Political Economy,* a group of stories on economic topics written for working people published in 1833. Unfortunately, its price made it too expensive for its intended market and it was not very successful.

In the same way that Maria Edgeworth drew upon her experience in raising her younger siblings in writing *Practical Education* with her father, Jane Marcet used her experience in writing stories and grammars for children. These included *Bertha's Visit to her Uncle in England* (1830), *Stories for Young Children* (1831), *Mary's Grammar* (1835), *Conversations for Children, on Land and Water* (1838), *Conversations on Language, for Children* (1844), *Willy's Grammar* (1845) and *Mrs Marcet's Story-book* (1858).

Writing in 1869, Harriet Martineau commented that:

The grandmammas of our time, however, declare with warmth, as do many mothers and governesses, that Mrs Marcet's very best books are her Stories for Very Little Children; *and certainly, judging by observation of many little children, those small volumes do appear to be unique in their suitableness to the minds they were addressed to. Mrs Barbauld's* Early Lessons *were good; Miss Edgeworth's were better; but Mrs Marcet's are transcendent, as far as they go.*[17]

Harriet Martineau dismissed works like *Mary's Grammar* as 'too much of the garrulous order'[17] although they were very successful. *The Literary Gazette* was more complimentary. In reviewing *Willy's Grammar* in 1845 it stated:

The plan is excellent, and the execution not less so. The infant mind is judiciously stimulated to inquiry; that inquiry is rewarded by information; that information is reiterated in new but not tiresome forms; and the understanding of the whole is tested by question and answer. To these are added suitable stories, which at once illustrate and impress the lesson, and entertain and improve the learner.[18]

The last few years
Jane's son Francis became a physicist and was elected a fellow of the Royal Society like his father before him. He worked closely with Arthur

Auguste de la Rive, whose brother Eugene married Jane's daughter Louisa in London in 1828 before settling in Geneva, Switzerland. Jane's other daughter Sophia married Edward Romilly, the son of Sir Samuel Romilly, and lived in England.

Jane spent the last years of her life living with her daughter Sophia in London. It would appear that the depression she had suffered from years before now took over her life. Harriet Martineau wrote that 'her nervous malady' had 'grievously prostrated her, it was understood, in her extreme old age.'[19] Jane died at her daughter Sophia's home in Stratton Street, Piccadilly, on 28 June 1858.

Jane's legacy
Jane Marcet may not have considered herself to be an original thinker, but she possessed the creativity and ability to present complicated concepts in a way that ordinary people could understand. Her *Conversations on Chemistry* helped get science on the curriculum for girls and was a major influence on Faraday's development as a scientist. Harriet Martineau wrote:

Mrs Marcet never made any false pretensions. She never overrated her own books, nor, consciously, her own knowledge. She sought information from learned persons, believed she understood what she was told, and generally did so; wrote down in a clear, cheerful, serviceable style what she had to tell; submitted it to criticism, accepted criticism gayly, and always protested against being ranked with authors of original quality, whether discoverers in science or thinkers in literature. She simply desired to be useful; and she was eminently so.[20]

Chapter 8

Engineering Enthusiast – Sarah Guppy (1770–1852)

Anyone visiting the city of Bristol must surely get at least a glimpse of the Clifton Suspension Bridge, the elegant marvel of Victorian engineering that has spanned the Avon Gorge since 1864. While we may take such massive structures for granted today, the bridge was, when built, a modern wonder. According to the plaque on the bridge, it was designed by one of the most famous engineers of the nineteenth century, Isambard Kingdom Brunel.

However, every great engineering project is a collaborative effort, and one of those who made a contribution to the Clifton Suspension Bridge was Bristol-based engineering enthusiast and Regency inventor, Sarah Guppy. Engineering historians disagree as to how much, if any, of the bridge design is attributable to Sarah, but there's no doubting that this inventive, if perhaps a little eccentric, woman offered a rare female perspective in an extremely masculine profession.

Engineering in the genes
Sarah's interest in how things worked probably began very early in life. She was born into an engineering family in Birmingham. We don't know exactly when she was born, but she was baptised on 5 November 1770. Her father, Richard Beach, ran a business making brass instruments and his brother, Thomas, made weighing equipment. His business was later taken over by Avery, a name still associated with the manufacture of scales today.

The family was reasonably wealthy and as she grew up, Sarah received a decent education, enabling her to pen a good letter, several of which have survived. We can only speculate over how much the young Sarah learned about her family's technical trade as she grew up, and whether

her interest was actively encouraged. But interested she was, as her later achievements proved.

In late Georgian Britain, the proper course for a young lady from a wealthy family was to marry. So on 22 February 1795, at the age of 24, Sarah married Samuel Guppy. Samuel was a Bristol merchant more than fifteen years older than her, whose business enterprises included brass and iron foundries and the manufacture of agricultural machinery. Sarah had moved from one engineering household to another.

Sarah clearly had a head for business. She took over all the correspondence for Samuel's firm and became his new business partner. The company offices were at 19 Poultry in the City of London, while the family home remained in Bristol, so it's likely she often travelled between the two cities.

Sarah and Samuel soon became parents. Their first child, Samuel, was born within ten months of the wedding and he was followed by five siblings in the years to 1809. The second son, Thomas Richard Guppy, inherited the family passion for engineering and became a close working partner of the Victorian engineering legend Isambard Kingdom Brunel. Together with Brunel, he established the Great Western Railway between Bristol and London and helped design ships, notably the SS *Great Western* and the SS *Great Britain*.

Sarah's first invention?

Sarah's interest in engineering was more than just a fascination with technical detail; she was also an innovator. Quite possibly, one of her first ideas created a fortune for her family, although, in accordance with Georgian expectations, her husband got the credit. In 1796, a year after his marriage to Sarah, Samuel Guppy patented a machine for cutting and finishing nails in a manner that would help sailing ships travel significantly faster. He patented some improvements to the machine in 1804. Living in the busy port city of Bristol, the Guppys would have fully understood the commercial advantages that came with cutting journey times on busy cargo routes.

Barnacles were a real problem for the wooden hulled ships of the day. These tiny creatures attached themselves in their thousands to the hull below the waterline, creating extra weight that slowed the ship down. It had been discovered that barnacles could be discouraged by nailing copper sheathing around the bottom of ships. However, though the copper sheathing successfully prevented barnacles attaching themselves to the hull, the rough heads of the metal nails that held the sheathing in place were still attracting the tiny creatures.

Guppy's patent was for a machine that solved this problem. It produced copper nails that were smooth headed and could be hammered down flush with the surface of the copper sheathing. This eliminated the protruding nail heads, reducing the volume of barnacles on a hull.

Keen to take advantage of this latest improvement, the Admiralty gave Guppy's Patent Sheathing Nail Manufactory a contract estimated to have been worth somewhere between £20,000 and £40,000. This was an extremely valuable agreement, equivalent to at least £1.5 to £3.1 million in today's money, based on the cost-of-living index, but worth as much as £18.7 to £37.4 million when relative wages are taken into account.[1]

But did Guppy really invent these machines, or were they actually the product of his wife's innovative thinking? According to family tradition, as passed down to Sarah's great granddaughter, Theodora Robinson, Sarah Guppy invented a way to apply copper plating to the bottom of ships to prevent barnacles for which the government had paid her £40,000. This sounds remarkably like Guppy's patent copper nails!

It's very probable that Sarah collaborated with her husband in technical aspects of his business. If they had batted ideas back and forth between them, the eventual solution could, quite genuinely, have been a joint effort. From the evidence we have today, there are strong indications that Sarah played a substantial part in arriving at this innovation, and in the subsequent negotiations with the Admiralty.

Stories and servants

Sarah was one of life's natural problem-solvers and she didn't allow her role as wife and mother to stifle her creativity. In 1800 she published a book of stories for children, with what we'd now consider a somewhat nannying title: *Instructive and Entertaining Dialogues for Children*.

The Monthly Review, a popular magazine of the time, described it as: 'Pretty little dialogues and illustrations, fitted to amuse and inform the mind in that early period for which they are immediately calculated. Any profits, which may accrue from the work, are destined to the use of a charity-school for girls at Bristol.'[2] That last sentence gives us an insight into Sarah's generous nature to those less fortunate than herself. The book enjoyed some success, reaching its fourteenth edition by 1833.

Not only did Sarah enjoy finding solutions to problems, she was also a woman with strong opinions and if she felt she could do some good, she made a point of sharing them. She seemed to have an innate belief in her own abilities, meaning that if she had an idea, it would profit others to hear it and pay attention.

In 1807, a tract entitled *Something that will interest the old and the young on the subject of female servants* was published and, though anonymous, Sarah is believed to be the author. The pamphlet discussed the surliness and bad behaviour of female servants and bemoaned the high wages they could earn which they then wasted on inappropriate dress that might lead them away from the path of virtue. The author called for a reduction in wages and urged ladies to be a good example to their female servants.

Sarah was a woman of action. Rather than just complaining about the unreliability and lack of morality in female servants, she also took positive action. During the Regency period, she was the main patron of the Society for the Reward and Encouragement of Virtuous, Faithful, and Industrious Female Servants – a group which she had founded. The society took a practical approach to the problem by setting up an employment agency in Bristol. Servants with good character references could register at the office and society members could go there to find reliable new household staff.

Sarah's solutions to public problems
While Sarah lived all her married life in Bristol, she would have occasionally travelled to and from London, to the offices of her husband's firm. While she was to become a fan of the new railways that began cutting across the nation later in her life, most of her travel would have been by coach, along turnpike roads.

Through her carriage window Sarah spotted what was, at least in her mind, a problem that needed a solution. She was concerned about the large piles of manure that farms had a habit of piling up alongside the roads and that were, in her view, going to waste. In 1811 Sarah felt moved to write to the agriculturalist Arthur Young, secretary of the Board of Agriculture, about it. She complained that the manure got 'wash'd away and goes only to nourish the noxious weeds in its neighbourhood'.[3]

Ever practical, Sarah had an engineering solution. She proposed a system of cisterns for storing manure at each farm so that it could be used as agricultural fertiliser. Not only did she suggest where these should be placed, but also how they should be built, including appropriate dimensions and the best materials to use for lining the cisterns to provide adequate drainage. It is not clear what Arthur Young thought of this helpful advice from a Bristol housewife.

In London, Sarah spied what was, again in her opinion, another problem that needed fixing. Smithfield Market had been used for the buying and selling of cattle for centuries, but during the nineteenth century, this noisy, smelly activity was growing rapidly in size to meet the demands of the increasing population of London. Its location, right in the centre of the city, was starting to cause concern, and Sarah felt compelled to share her views in a letter, sent to Robert Jenkinson, 2nd Earl of Liverpool, in 1811.

Sarah's main concern was about congestion. She wrote that proposals to keep the Smithfield cattle market where it was would be 'endangering the lives of Pedestrians, and preventing Carriages of all descriptions from motion for a considerable time together.'[4] She was also unhappy about the long distance that the animals had to be driven through the streets before they were slaughtered, causing them to be feverish and distressed. Her suggestion was to create six district cattle markets which could be open every day, three miles out of the city in each direction.

Another recommendation Sarah made was to take as much land as could be spared from the Haymarket and turn it into a green space, which would be both profitable to the city and beneficial to its populace. By converting this area into a garden and charging a subscription to each housekeeper in the city it could become 'a place of resort and emolument and rendering it a source of health and recreation, much wanted.'[4]

A campaign to relocate Smithfield Market did eventually develop, although it did not gather momentum until some thirty years after Sarah wrote her letter. In a postscript, Sarah expressed her concern for the animals – a very unusual sentiment at the time as interest in animal welfare was very much in its infancy. The Society for the Prevention of Cruelty to Animals, later the Royal Society for the Prevention of Cruelty to Animals when it received Queen Victoria's patronage, was the world's first charity devoted to animal welfare and it was not founded until 1824, more than a decade after Sarah's letter.

Sarah wrote that she had not mentioned 'the sufferings of the poor animals because man where his interest, and convenience is served, (generally speaking) feels little for any animal, but if observed their eyes sufficiently indicate that they do severely suffer both in mind and body.'[4] Clearly she did not appreciate her advice being ignored as she wrote again on the same matter in 1814.

On building bridges
For all her opinions on agricultural matters and stories for children, Sarah was first and foremost an engineer, and an inventive one at that. She may have allowed her husband to take all the credit for the invention of the machine to create copper headed nails, but on 4 March 1811 she registered, in her own name, a patent for bridge building.

It is through this patent that Sarah could well have influenced the design of the famous Clifton Suspension Bridge. It's even more likely that it contributed to the Menai Suspension Bridge in Wales, built by Thomas Telford.

The patent was granted to 'Sarah Guppy, wife of Samuel Guppy, in the City of Bristol, merchant; for a mode of erecting and constructing bridges and rail roads without arches or sterlings, whereby the danger of being washed away by floods is avoided.'[5]

Put simply, the invention was a design for a suspension bridge. Her technique was to use 'a row of piles, with suitable framing' on each side of the place over which the bridge was to be built and then to employ strong metal chains fixed to the tops of the masonry structures in order to support a platform on which a road or railway could be built.[5] Sarah wasn't inventing the first suspension bridge – that had been designed and built in Jacob's Creek, Pennsylvania, USA, in 1801 by Irish-born James Finley – but her method of safe piling was innovative.

Sarah Guppy was entered into the *Oxford Dictionary of National Biography* for the first time in April 2016 and in her entry, Professor Madge Dresser claimed that 'Both Thomas Telford and Isambard Kingdom Brunel utilized the principles of Sarah Guppy's 1811 patent in their respective designs for the Menai and Clifton suspension bridges.'[6] This led to dramatic headlines claiming that Sarah deserved credit for these structures. Other writers tried to eliminate her influence altogether by saying that the designs for these bridges didn't incorporate her ideas at all.

This controversy wasn't new. Back in 1839, an article in the *Bristol Mercury* had cited Sarah's patent and reported that, when approached by

Thomas Telford whilst working on his design for the Menai Suspension Bridge, she had given him permission to use the design free of charge. Apparently she believed the invention was for the public benefit and so would not charge a fee for using her idea.

In 1860, engineers were still arguing, in *The Mechanics' Magazine*, about who deserved credit for the first modern chain suspension bridge in Britain. It was pointed out that the Menai Suspension Bridge was not the first such construction, as Captain Sir Samuel Brown's Union Bridge over the Tweed had been finished six years earlier in 1820. The writer then went on to give credit to Sarah Guppy for the idea 'about the time that the late lamented engineers, Stephenson and Brunel, were at school' and that she had 'not only designed a chain suspension bridge, but declared it possible to carry railroads over rivers by that means; and I feel quite confident the gallant general will not be so ungallant as to attempt to wrest the credit of suggesting the use of chains from our fair countrywoman.'[7]

As with the nail making machine, the truth is that innovation and design is a collaborative process. Sarah Guppy was a woman operating at the highest level in a man's world. It is probable that Telford did ask permission to use Sarah's design, whether he actually employed it or not. There is no doubt that Brunel would have talked about bridges with Sarah, as the two families knew each other well. Sarah's son Thomas became one of Brunel's closest working partners. Family tradition says that Sarah made models of Brunel's designs.

Sarah remained interested in bridge building long after registering her patent. She was said to have spent many hours working on plans for a bridge to span the Avon Gorge, but when a competition was launched to find a winning design, she failed to submit an entry. Perhaps she felt her design was not suitable, or maybe she was reluctant to push herself into public view.

Domestic problems
It is easy to forget, from our twenty-first century perspective, that in Sarah's time, women were expected to concern themselves mainly with domestic matters. She was not idle in that sphere either. Again, she spotted a problem that needed a solution, in the form of wasted heat in hot water boilers used for making drinks. In 1812 she patented her invention for 'improvements in tea and coffee urns'.[8] Her idea was to add extra vessels

to the top of the urn in order to use the heat from the boiling water to boil eggs and keep toast warm. Instead of just providing a hot drink, the urn would thereby deliver an entire hot breakfast! Sarah was clearly proud of her invention as below the patent description she observed: 'The superior utility of these urns is so very evident, that it is quite unnecessary to say any thing in their favour – they speak for themselves.'[9]

In 1814, Sarah wrote a tract entitled *Considerations with the sketch of a plan for providing suitable, agreeable and permanent residences for ladies.* Sarah was concerned about the plight of respectable women who had insufficient means, and in this tract, she laid out proposals for a housing scheme to provide homes for impoverished, but upright women.

Around this time, another problem was brewing in Sarah's life. It seems that her marriage to Samuel was struggling. An inheritance from Sarah's father allowed Samuel to retire from business and from 1817, it is his son Thomas whose name appears on the office leases and London directories for the patent copper nail manufactory. According to the story passed down through the family, having made his will in 1817, in which he left everything to 'my beloved wife Sarah Guppy', Samuel left his wife and family and went to end his days with his sister, Ann, in Somerset.[10]

It is impossible to tell why Samuel left, but he may have felt inadequate compared to his socially able, highly intelligent wife. She was said to have a fiery temper, so she may not have been easy to live with. But, while it is possible to sympathise with the difficulties of living with genius, it seems harsh that he abdicated his role as head of the household when his youngest child was only 9. Samuel may have thought he was going to die soon, but he lived for another thirteen years. He was buried in Chard, Somerset, on 20 May 1830.

Sarah's inventiveness continued into widowhood, with another patent in 1831. This time, her invention was for an exercise bed. The special features of the bed were designed to make it suitable for an invalid. The first addition was to make it easy for an invalid to get into bed by means of a chest of drawers with sliding covers which could be pulled out and used as steps up to the bed. The second feature was a valance round the frame at the top of the bed which could be arranged so as 'to regulate the circulation, for more or less, according to the temperature of the room, or the state of the person in bed.'[11] The third was an intriguing system of pulleys by which a sick person could exercise in bed. *The Repertory of Patent Inventions* ended its description with the words: 'We should have been glad if the tomb-like appearance of English beds had been avoided: but as it is, the improvements of Sarah Guppy are acceptable; and, combined with other arrangements already well known, may soothe the body of pain, and lighten the heart of sorrow.'[11]

During her life in Bristol, Sarah lived at various houses. She lived in Queen's Square with Samuel and then, from about 1820, she lived at Arnos Vale Court in Brislington. By 1831, she had moved to Richmond Hill in Clifton. She resided first at number 6, which was called Farway House, and then after, at the building next door, number 7, named Mornington House.

Even in her own home, Sarah's passion for invention was evident. Her house had one of the earliest domestic lifts installed and she also erected a covered walkway from the pavement to the front door so that ladies would not soil their dresses if they arrived at the house when it was raining.

Railway enthusiast

Sarah was a great advocate for the railway and in 1835, she wrote a letter to the press extolling the blessings brought about by the Great Western Railway which had been founded two years previously with her son Thomas as the largest investor and later director.

By 1837, she had invested in the Bath and Weymouth Great Western Union Railway to the tune of £2,000. She also had shares in the Bristol and Gloucestershire Extension Railway worth almost another £2,000. She frequently wrote letters to the railway authorities. In 1841, she wrote expressing her concern about landslides on railway banks and suggested planting poplar trees as a way to combat this problem. She also suggested to the Great Western Railway authorities that they should purchase the Bristol and Gloucester line.

A woman of science and charity

Sarah was never one to confine herself to the home but was always looking to contribute to the wider community. She financed a project to turn a warehouse on Bristol dockside into a shelter for seamen and supported both the Bristol Dispensary for the Relief of the Sick Poor and a charity to help the blind.

Sarah did not seem to be bothered that she was a woman in a man's environment. It didn't stop her buying a share in the Bristol Institution for the Advancement of Science in 1836, or becoming the only female member of the Bristol horticultural society. She even ventured, briefly, into publishing, becoming a partner in a local newspaper, the *Bristol Mercury*, until 1837.

An unwise marriage

By the mid-1830s, Sarah had a new problem in her life. She was lonely. Years later, her great-granddaughter remembered her mother saying that Sarah was 'a lonely old woman living alone in that great, gloomy Faraway House [sic].'[12]

This is where Sarah's problem solving abilities seem to have let her down. It is reported that Charles Eyre Coote, a man almost thirty years younger than Sarah, then in her sixties, spied her going about her business in Bristol one day; on being told she was a wealthy widow, he announced his intention of marrying her. Whatever the truth of this story, the couple wed – without the knowledge of her family – on 29 January 1837.

What on earth possessed the wealthy Sarah Guppy to get married again? She was 66 years old, had been a widow for seven years – and probably living as one for even longer. Instead of choosing a dependable widower of her own age, she selected as her husband a man barely half her age, whom she must have suspected was a fortune hunter.

All the evidence suggests that Coote was indeed after Sarah's money. He did an effective job of squandering her fortune in the years that followed their wedding. Like many of his contemporaries, Coote was expensive to keep and had an unfortunate predilection for gambling. When Sarah died in 1852, her once sizeable estate was valued at a mere £500. When her husband collapsed and died just a year later, it had dwindled further to just £200.

Some reports suggest that the couple didn't live together, but on both the 1841 and 1851 censuses, they are registered as both residing in the same house on Richmond Hill, Bristol.

Sarah's last years

Sarah continued to be active and inventive into her seventies. In 1841, she wrote a letter to the Royal Agricultural Society with her recommendations on how to cure foot rot in sheep using a remedy based on tobacco. Her letter was read out at one of their meetings where she was commended for her readiness to put forward her ideas for anything in the public interest.

Charles Eyre Coote filed a patent for a fire extinguisher in 1842. It was his first and only patent and was almost definitely invented by Sarah. Why it was filed in his name, rather than hers, is a mystery. Perhaps, as with what was probably her first invention (the nail machine), her husband felt it should be in his name.

For years, Sarah seemingly devoted herself to domestic improvements. She patented inventions for a candlestick that increased the burning time of candles; a portable oven; a fire hood for stoves; a plate warmer; and a ventilating pillar. In 1844, she filed her last patent, once more contributing to the wider community by patenting some improvements in caulking boats.

Sarah died at her home on Richmond Hill on 24 August 1852 and was buried at St Andrew's Churchyard in Clifton, Bristol. Her obituary in the *Bristol Mercury* described her as 'a lady of a most active and enterprising mind' who was 'ever animated by a strong desire to be of service to the age in which she lived. The study of mechanics and chemistry and the science of agriculture engaged much of her attention' and 'she early enunciated the principal of suspension bridges, for which, as long ago as 1811, she took out the first patent ever granted, and there are other utile matters which may be traced to her suggestive mind.'[13]

Interestingly, Sarah was also given a substantial mention in the obituary of her son Thomas in the same paper in 1882: 'Mr Guppy no doubt inherited much of his mechanical bias and inventive genius from his mother.' It continued: 'She was a lady of remarkable ability, and made some inventions, and it may be mentioned incidentally that to her energy and influence the public are indebted for the open space, now used as a flower nursery by Mr Baskerville, which lies between Richmond Hill and the Queen's Road.'[14]

Sarah's legacy

The open space referred to in her son's obituary is a small legacy that has stretched into the twenty-first century. Sarah bought some land opposite to her houses on Richmond Hill, which she wanted to be kept as a green space within the city for the enjoyment of the people of Clifton. Sarah had long been convinced of the benefits of recreational spaces in cities. Part of the land was planted with trees and shrubs, and part was turned into a nursery garden. It is controlled by Bristol City Council, who attempted to turn it into a car park in the 1990s. There is still an area kept as a landscaped garden today, however.

Sarah Guppy was a woman with a truly inventive mind at a time when women and engineering did not mix. Her many inventions may have come and gone, but her contribution to the creative mix in which the designs for two of Britain's greatest suspension bridges were made should not be forgotten. While the Clifton Suspension Bridge in Bristol bears the name of Isambard Kingdom Brunel, it is, at least for some of us, a visual reminder of Sarah Guppy and her engineering creativity.

Chapter 9

Mr Darcy's Maker – Jane Austen (1775–1817)

The Regency was invented by a witty, observant young woman from Hampshire. Or it can feel like that. Our image of Regency England – a land of grand houses, romantic intrigues and Empire line dresses – is plucked directly from the pages of Jane Austen's novels. Or at least, from their representations in film and television.

It is perhaps surprising, then, to discover that Jane's books, though popular in her lifetime, did not look as though they were going to last. They did not stir enough emotion for early Victorians and it wasn't until fifty years after her death that Jane's talent was again widely recognised. Today, 'Jane Austen appreciation' has become a worldwide industry.

Early life and education
Jane Austen spent her first twenty-five years living in rural Hampshire. She was born on 16 December 1775 in Steventon, where her father, George Austen, was the rector.

George had done rather well for himself. His father had only been a surgeon and, however skilled a vocation this was, it lay outside the acceptable professions of the gentry – the church, the law and the army or navy. George owed his rise in status to the generosity of his relations. His uncle, Francis Austen, paid for his education, and a distant cousin, Thomas Knight, gave him the living at Steventon. On top of this, George had married well. Jane's mother, Cassandra Leigh, came from a family of landed gentry and was related to the Leighs of Stoneleigh Abbey.

Family was extremely important to Jane. Hers was large – she had six brothers and a sister. James, the eldest, was of a studious nature. He became a clergyman and took over the living at Steventon when his father retired. Next came George, who was disabled in some way and did not

117

live at home. Edward was fortunate enough to attract the interest of the childless Thomas Knight, who adopted him and made him his heir. Henry was the most volatile of Jane's brothers. He joined the army, but when that didn't suit, he went into banking. When his bank failed, he became a rector. Francis and Charles both went into the navy where they excelled, both rising to the rank of admiral. Cassandra was two years older than Jane and the only other girl in the family. The two sisters were inseparable; they shared a bedroom and had their own little sitting room.

Whilst Jane was still very young, about 7 years old, she was sent away to Oxford, with her sister Cassandra and their cousin Jane Cooper, to be educated by Mrs Cawley, a distant family connection. It must have been very hard on the girls to be torn from the home they loved, but perhaps their father felt unqualified to educate his girls as appropriately as his sons. The experience was nearly the death of them.

Without warning, Mrs Cawley – to whom the girls had taken an immediate dislike – moved to Southampton, where Jane and Cassandra became seriously ill with a putrid fever – probably what we would now call typhus. For some reason, Mrs Cawley did not see fit to inform their parents. Fortunately, Jane Cooper did. She wrote and told her mother that her cousins were extremely unwell. The girls were immediately removed from Mrs Cawley's care and nursed at home. Jane was so ill that she almost died. Jane Cooper's poor mother was less fortunate; she caught the infection and it proved fatal.

Not long after, a second attempt was made at sending the girls away to be educated, but this was equally unsuccessful. The girls were well cared for at the Abbey House School in Reading, but their timetable of lessons was so sparse that there was more time for reading novels than learning. Whether George Austen realised this, or whether he was short of money, or whether he just wanted his girls living under his own roof again is not clear but, by the end of 1786, Jane and Cassandra had returned to Steventon. Both girls lived in the family home for the rest of their lives.

This was not the end of their education, however. George Austen gave his daughters the run of his extensive library, which Jane in particular made good use of. Her studious brother James helped to guide her reading.

The Steventon years
Soon after Jane had returned home for good, she began writing. Her father

encouraged her, providing plenty of paper for her scribblings, and giving her notebooks in which to copy out her best work. These early writings are known as her 'juvenilia'. They include plays and short novels in letter form, like *Love and Friendship*, and the comical *The History of England*, illustrated by Cassandra. Jane also wrote a short novel called *Lady Susan* – a story whose central character was both titled and wicked, most unlike her later work.

Jane's life was not full of drama; it was the quiet life of a moderately wealthy family of gentry living in the country. Most of her activities were focused on the home, in a daily routine shared with her close-knit family and a few intimate friends. She helped supervise the servants, played the piano, read and wrote. Her favourite novel was Samuel Richardson's *Sir Charles Grandison,* and as a young woman she wrote a play based on it. She was also an accomplished needlewoman.

In the evenings, the Austens entertained themselves by engaging in stimulating conversation and reading novels aloud to each other. Jane frequently read from her own work, discussing the plot and characters with her family. They played games – card and board games and word games like charades – and performed amateur theatricals.

As well as their immediate family, the Austens were particularly friendly with George Austen's widowed sister, Philadelphia Hancock, and her flirtatious daughter Eliza. Jane's particular friends included Martha Lloyd, a daughter of the rector of a neighbouring parish, and Madam Lefroy, the wife of the rector of Ashe, as well as Elizabeth, Catherine, and Alethea Bigg-Wither of Manydown Park near Basingstoke.

Jane and Cassandra often stayed at Manydown Park when they attended the monthly assemblies in Basingstoke where Jane had the chance to indulge her passion for dancing, which she was apparently very good at. Her domestic routine was punctuated by trips away visiting family and friends, sometimes with Cassandra. It is fortunate for us that Jane and Cassandra were not always in the same place because it is Jane's letters, most especially those to her sister, which give us the best insights into what she was really like.

Jane regularly visited Bath where her cousins the Coopers had a house, and where her uncle James Leigh-Perrot lived with his wife for part of the year. They visited Edward at the home of the Knights – Godmersham Park in Kent – and the Leigh-Perrots at Scarlets, their estate in Berkshire.

Although Jane's life was centred on her home, she was not ignorant of events abroad. She was keenly interested in how the war against France progressed because her naval brothers were at sea. The impact of the French Revolution on her family was even more disturbing. Her charming cousin Eliza Hancock had married a French nobleman, Jean Capot de Feuillide, and in 1794, during the Reign of Terror, this unfortunate man was sent to the guillotine. Three years later, Eliza married Jane's brother Henry.

Even life in England could be unpleasant if you got on the wrong side of the law. This was brought home very keenly to the Austen family in 1799 when Jane's aunt, the wealthy Mrs Leigh-Perrot, was falsely accused of shoplifting. Although innocent, she spent months in jail awaiting trial, before being completely acquitted. If she had been found guilty, she could have been transported to Botany Bay, or worse, sentenced to death.

Affairs of the heart

Although neither Jane nor Cassandra ever married, their lives were not without love. In 1795, Cassandra became engaged to the Reverend Thomas Fowle. Tom was well known to the Austen family as he had been one of the students their father had tutored. There is no doubt that Jane approved of her sister's choice. Tom was not yet in a position to marry, but his prospects were good, because he had been promised a well-paid church appointment in the future by his patron, Lord Craven. In the meantime, the family decided to keep news of Tom and Cassandra's engagement to themselves.

Lord Craven was about to travel to the West Indies and offered to take Tom with him as his private chaplain. Convinced it was in their best interests to do so, Tom agreed, but in 1797, tragedy struck. Tom became ill with yellow fever on his way home and died. Cassandra was heartbroken. What made matters even worse was that Lord Craven said he would never have taken Tom with him if he had known of the engagement. Although I am sure it did not soften the blow at the time, Tom left Cassandra £1,000 in his will.

Jane was not lacking in admirers. Whilst Cassandra was away visiting, she began a flirtation of her own. The gentleman in question was another Thomas – Tom Lefroy – a nephew of her good friend Madam Lefroy. Jane described him in a letter to her sister in January 1796: 'He is a very gentlemanlike, good-looking, pleasant young man.'[1]

Jane clearly liked this phrase. She used it no less than eight times in

Pride and Prejudice, which she started writing in its early form – *First Impressions* – at this time. In it, she described Mr Bingley as 'good-looking and gentlemanlike' but criticised Mr Darcy for not behaving 'in a more gentlemanlike manner'.[2, 3]

The attraction between Jane and Tom was strong enough to cause his aunt some concern. It would have been an imprudent match. There was no money on either side. Tom was to practise law in Ireland and if he was going to be successful, his marriage needed to bring him money or connections, or preferably both.

It is hard to tell how much they saw of each other after their initial meeting or how serious their feelings for each other were, but one of Jane's letters suggests that she was still interested in Tom two years later. Conscious of Madam Lefroy's disapproval, she didn't dare ask after him.

Tom was sent back to Ireland. Although he admitted to his nephew later in life that he had been in love with Jane, it was only short-lived. He was married just a year later and went on to become Lord Chief Justice of Ireland.

Madam Lefroy was eager to promote an alternative suitor to her young friend – the Reverend Samuel Blackall, a young fellow of Emmanuel College, Cambridge. But after the gentlemanlike demeanour of Tom Lefroy, Samuel Blackall seemed as pompous and uninteresting to Jane as Mr Collins seemed to Elizabeth Bennet after she had enjoyed a flirtation with Mr Wickham in *Pride and Prejudice*.

Life in Bath

In November 1800, Jane's father suddenly announced his intention to leave Hampshire. He had decided to hand over the living at Steventon to his eldest son, James, and move with his wife and daughters to Bath. Jane and Cassandra were shocked. Steventon was the only home that either of them had ever known. They moved into a house opposite Sydney Gardens: 4 Sydney Place. Though they were living in a different place and their friends were far away, the routine of their lives carried on much as before. They attended balls in the Assembly Rooms and visited the circulating library in Milsom Street.

During the summer, they sublet the house and went visiting friends and family, or took lodgings by the seaside. According to Cassandra, it was during one of these summer visits that Jane met the love of her life. Whilst staying at the seaside, possibly in Sidmouth, Jane encountered a gentleman who was very taken with her. We have no record of his name, but Jane was very attracted to her admirer who was said to have been handsome, charming and intelligent – no doubt what Jane would have called gentlemanlike. The details are frustratingly sparse. The young gentleman may, or may not, have been a clergyman. But one thing is certain – the ending was not happy. A short while later, Jane learned that he had died.

The proposal
In November 1802, Jane and Cassandra returned to Steventon to stay at the parsonage with their brother James before paying a visit to their friends the Bigg-Withers at Manydown Park.

Whilst at Manydown Park, something of a surprising nature took place: Jane received a proposal of marriage. What is even more surprising is that she accepted. The proposal came from their friend's 21-year-old brother, Harris Bigg-Wither, heir to the Manydown estate. This was Jane's opportunity to secure her future and provide a home for herself and her beloved sister in their old age. It would have been a marriage of convenience on her side at least. Overnight, she changed her mind. Perhaps she couldn't get her parents' happy marriage out of her head, or found the comparison with her lost love too stark. Perhaps she simply realised that she could not live with him after all. Harris was plain and unattractive without much conversation, and she may have doubted her ability to respect someone whom she had grown up with as the younger brother of her friends. Harris probably had no idea how important writing was to her and maybe she feared that marriage would be the end of her writing aspirations.

On a more basic level, she may have been scared of dying in childbirth – a very common occurrence in late Georgian England. Whatever her reasons, she broke off their engagement the next morning and returned to her brother's house in deep distress. But even Steventon was too near the scene of her embarrassment. She had to get away. She begged James to take her and Cassandra back to Bath without delay, even though he would be unable to get back in time to take the services on Sunday. So ended Jane Austen's short-lived betrothal.

A change in circumstances
In the autumn of 1804, the Austens moved to 3 Green Park Buildings.

Jane then embarked upon one of the saddest periods in her life. In December, she received news that her dear friend Madam Lefroy had been killed after falling from her horse. Worse was to come. The following month, Jane's father died after a short illness.

Overcome by grief, they also had to contend with reduced circumstances. Mrs Austen and her daughters were left with very little to live on and had to rely on the generosity of Jane's brothers to top up their income.

At first they stayed in Bath as Mrs Austen thought it would be advantageous to remain in the same town as the Leigh-Perrots. They found cheaper lodgings to reduce their overheads, first in Gay Street and then in Trim Street. Their friend Martha Lloyd had also suffered a bereavement. Her mother had died leaving her homeless and so the Austens invited her to live with them.

Jane did not want to stay in Bath where her beloved father had died. Fortunately, Jane's mother was persuaded to move to Southampton where they shared a home in Castle Square with Jane's brother Frank and his new wife.

Life in Chawton

Edward soon devised a longer-term solution for looking after his mother and sisters, offering them a house on either one of his estates – Chawton in Hampshire or Godmersham Park in Kent. There probably was not much competition. Going back to rural Hampshire where they had been so happy for so many years was the obvious choice.

The Austens, together with Martha Lloyd, moved into a cottage in the village of Chawton, near Alton in Hampshire, in the summer of 1809 and Jane lived there until just before she died. Jane was a fond aunt and was particularly close to James's eldest daughter, Anna Austen, and Edward's eldest daughter, Fanny Knight.

It was during these years at Chawton Cottage that Jane's hopes as an author began to be realised. Jane spent many hours writing, sitting at her desk in the drawing room, with a view through the window and a squeaky door which gave her warning of interruptions so she could hide her manuscript from visitors.

Despite the fact that Jane was writing throughout most of her adult life, she only completed six novels. Whilst at Chawton, she rewrote two of her earliest works and created three new ones.

Jane's novels

The first three of Jane's novels all started out with different titles from those under which they were eventually published. The first version of *Sense and Sensibility* was probably written as a series of letters and was started in about 1793, when Jane was still a teenager. Back then, it was known by the names of the two heroines, *Elinor and Marianne*. Having been completely rewritten, it was accepted for publication at the author's risk by Thomas Egerton of London and was published anonymously as 'By a Lady' in 1811.[4]

Pride and Prejudice started life as *First Impressions*. It was submitted for publication in 1797, but was rejected. However, after her success with *Sense and Sensibility*, Jane was able to sell the copyright of *Pride and Prejudice* to Egerton for the sum of £110. Unfortunately, this proved to be a poor financial decision. It was published anonymously in 1813 as 'By the author of *Sense and Sensibility*' and was very successful, but Jane received no more money for her most popular work, as Egerton scooped all the profits.[5]

Jane was immensely fond of the main characters of *Pride and Prejudice* and wrote to her sister that it was enough for her if people liked Elizabeth Bennet. She wrote that she had failed to find her picture but had discovered one of Mrs Bingley. Clearly it was a habit with her to look for artistic representations of her characters and she had found what she thought looked like Jane Bennet, later Mrs Bingley, in an exhibition in London, though she had failed to find one that looked like Elizabeth Bennet.

Jane's third book was *Northanger Abbey*, a story poking fun at the popular Gothic novel. Known by the title *Susan*, it was sold to the publisher Crosby in 1803 for £10. Jane waited and waited, but Crosby did not print her book. Why the publisher invested in an unknown author and then failed to print is a mystery. Crosby agreed to sell the copyright back to Jane for the £10 he had paid for it. Needless to say, he was surely dismayed when he realised that the copyright he resold for such a paltry sum in 1816 was for a book by the author of *Pride and Prejudice*.

Once her manuscript was back under her control, Jane changed the heroine's name from Susan to Catherine because of a clash with a recent publication. She wrote an introduction to the book explaining that publication had been delayed for a number of years since the story had been written. Regrettably, she did not live to see it in print. It was finally published after her death under the name chosen by her brother – *Northanger Abbey.*

Between writing *Susan* and beginning *Mansfield Park*, Jane started the story of *The Watsons*. Sadly, she abandoned work on it, perhaps feeling that her own situation was too close to that of the Watson sisters for comfort. Her father was elderly like Mr Watson and when her father died, she found she could not continue with it. All that we are left with is a fragment, and hints of the plot that had been talked about within the family.

Jane started writing *Mansfield Park* at the beginning of the Regency period in 1811. It was the first new story she had begun since her father's death and the writing style reflected her more mature view on life. It centred on Fanny Price, a girl removed from her birth home to that of a wealthier relation – in effect, what had happened to her brother Edward, though he was adopted and made Thomas Knight's heir, whereas Fanny was treated as the poor relation. Jane drew on her own experience of keeping up with her brothers while they were at sea to add real depth to Fanny's relationship with her sailor brother William. It was published on commission by Egerton in 1814 and was the most financially successful of her books during her lifetime, earning her at least £320.

After *Mansfield Park* came another story based on life in a big house in the country: *Emma*. The house was Hartfield, home of Emma Woodhouse, the eponymous heroine. Jane made Emma intelligent, rich, and rather inclined to get her own way. Instead of worshipping the ground upon which the heroine walked, the hero, Mr Knightley, was apt to criticise her behaviour in an attempt to improve her. It is her father who sees her as perfection and who feels that marriages break up the family circle. How much was Jane writing from her own feelings here? And what of the words she puts into Emma Woodhouse's mouth on the prospect of being an ageing spinster?

'A single woman, with a very narrow income, must be a ridiculous, disagreeable old maid ... but a single woman, of good fortune, is always respectable, and may be as sensible and pleasant as any body else.'[6]

In 1815, whilst Jane was in London seeing her new publisher, John Murray, about the publication of *Emma*, her brother Henry suddenly became very ill. During the short-lived crisis, one of the Prince Regent's physicians was consulted. Knowing that the regent was a big fan of Jane's books and kept a copy of her works at each of his residences, he felt it was his duty to let the regent know that Jane was in London.

As a result, Jane was invited by the regent's librarian, the Reverend James Stanier Clarke, to visit Carlton House. The prince was not at home, but Clarke had been told to show her every courtesy. He also hinted that the regent would be happy for her to dedicate a future novel to him. Jane did not approve of the regent's profligate lifestyle, but Clarke's 'suggestion' was little short of a royal command. When *Emma* was published in December 1815, it included a dedication to the Prince Regent.

Almost as soon as she had finished *Emma*, she started writing her last complete novel, *The Elliots*, later known as *Persuasion*. Perhaps she realised that her time was running out. *Persuasion* looks at the themes of second chances and hopeless love – themes that she had examined many years before in *Sense and Sensibility*. The book drew on Jane's experience of Bath and Lyme Regis. The heroine, Anne Elliot, shares some of Jane's own feelings. Anne dislikes Bath because of the associations with the death of her mother; Jane's memories of Bath were coloured by the death of her father. On the other hand, Jane had happy memories of Lyme Regis and gave these feelings to Anne who also loved the place.

Surely it was observing her sister's undiminished attachment to her fiancé after his death over the long years that followed that enabled Jane to create such a genuine character as Anne Elliot in *Persuasion*. Anne's words echoed what Jane must have seen was true, that women lived 'at home, quiet, confined, and our feelings prey upon us.'[7] What heartache is summed up in Anne's earnest effusion? 'All the privilege I claim for my own sex (it is not a very enviable one; you need not covet it), is that of loving longest, when existence or when hope is gone.'[7]

More than in any of her other books, we see evidence of Jane's intimate knowledge of the navy through her closeness with her naval brothers, Frank and Charles.

Jane's illness and death

In the autumn of 1816, Jane became very ill. Nevertheless, early in 1817, she was well enough to start writing another novel – *The Brothers*. It was a story that poked fun at the craze for the seaside and revolved around the fanatical Mr Parker who was determined to establish his own seaside resort at Sanditon – the name by which it later became known.

126

By this time, Jane was fading fast. By March she was too weak to write and had to abandon *Sanditon* after writing just twelve tantalising chapters. It remained, like *The Watsons*, a fragment. It is difficult to tell exactly what Jane was suffering from. For a long time, it has been generally accepted that she was dying of Addison's disease, but it may have been the result of an underlying condition of tuberculosis or cancer.

Whatever it was that was making Jane ill, it was fatal. Despite moving to Winchester in May to be closer to expert medical advice, there was nothing that anyone could do for her. Jane died in Winchester on 18 July 1817. Through Henry's connections with the church, he was able to arrange for Jane to be buried at Winchester Cathedral where her memorial gravestone can still be seen today.

In December 1817, Jane's final two complete novels were published in a joint edition: *Northanger Abbey* and *Persuasion*, with a brief biographical note written by her brother Henry. For the first time, Jane Austen was credited as the author.

What was Jane really like?
In 1869, Jane's nephew, Edward Austen-Leigh, published the first biography of Jane: *A Memoir of Jane Austen*. This was Jane Austen as her family wanted her to be seen, as a good-natured, loving, spinster aunt, without ambition for fame or fortune, who fitted the image of Victorian respectability. Her nephew wrote:

> *In person she was very attractive; her figure was rather tall and slender, her step light and firm, and her whole appearance expressive of health and animation. In complexion she was a clear brunette with a rich colour; she had full round cheeks, with mouth and nose small and well formed, bright hazel eyes, and brown hair forming natural curls close round her face. If not so regularly handsome as her sister, yet her countenance had a peculiar charm of its own to the eyes of most beholders.*[8]

In 1913, a second biography was published: *Jane Austen: Her Life and Letters – A Family Record*. It was written by two more Austen descendants, William Austen-Leigh and Richard Arthur Austen-Leigh. The authors used family papers and letters to produce a much more rounded picture of Jane.

Frustratingly, there is only one verified likeness of Jane Austen in existence – an amateur sketch by her sister, Cassandra, in about 1810, which her family did not think was very good. Desperate to know what Jane really looked like, in 2002, the Jane Austen Centre in Bath commissioned Melissa Dring, a forensic artist, to create a new portrait of Jane Austen. Starting with Cassandra's sketch, Dring used eye-witness accounts and pictures of Jane's family to produce a new portrait. Whilst acknowledging that the image is partly speculative, Dring believes that there is a good chance it is something like the real Jane Austen. Dring's portrait was then used as the basis for a waxwork by sculptor Mark Richards which was unveiled at the Jane Austen Centre in 2014.

Jane's legacy
Jane Austen left us with six complete novels, together with two novel fragments and various other short works, mostly written in her youth. Many think her novels are exceptional, but that was not always the case. Shortly after her death, Jane's books went out of print and although they were reprinted in the 1830s, they were only read by the discerning few. They lacked the powerful emotion that the Victorians generally looked for in a novel.

It wasn't until the 1880s that Jane Austen's works returned to popularity. The publication of Jane's first biography in 1869 generated new interest in her novels from both literary critics and regular readers. By the end of the century, her books had been translated into other languages and were available in a variety of editions, including, importantly, inexpensive popular versions.

The literary elite felt that the masses could not appreciate Jane's works as they could and, in 1894, George Saintsbury, a literary historian and critic, coined the term 'Janeite', meaning someone who could properly appreciate the work of Jane Austen. Although some Janeites today are serious literary admirers of Jane Austen's writings, the term has also come to mean quite the opposite. Today, most Janeites not only embrace Jane's writings, but her person and period as well.

So how did the modern-day Janeite evolve? The journey probably began around 1940 when the first film version of *Pride and Prejudice* was released starring Laurence Olivier and Greer Garson. In the same year, the Jane Austen Society was established and, in 1947, the Jane Austen Memorial Trust successfully bought Chawton Cottage and founded the Jane Austen's House Museum, which continues to draw thousands of Jane Austen enthusiasts to its doors.

1995 was a landmark year with the release of the BBC's brilliant dramatisation of *Pride and Prejudice* starring Colin Firth as Mr Darcy, and Emma Thompson's award winning film adaptation of *Sense and Sensibility*. Suddenly Austen's works were reaching an audience who had not read any of her books. This was further fuelled by the 2005 film of *Pride and Prejudice* starring Keira Knightley.

The surge in popularity for Jane Austen, and the Regency world she described so deftly, has inspired a wealth of Austen-related activities and tributes. The first Jane Austen Festival in Bath was held in September 2001, with its first Regency costumed promenade in 2004, comprising just thirty people. The event now attracts Jane Austen fans from around the globe and in 2014, a world-record-breaking 550 Austen enthusiasts paraded through the streets of Bath in Regency costume

The popularity of Jane Austen is exemplified by the story of a ring that once belonged to her. In 2012, American singer Kelly Clarkson bought the ring for an incredible £152,450, but was refused permission to take the ring out of the United Kingdom on the basis that it was a national treasure. Jane Austen's House Museum successfully raised the money to repurchase the ring through crowdfunding and displayed it for the first time on 14 February 2014.

Jane Austen is now so well known, and so closely associated with our nation's heritage, that the Bank of England chose her to feature on the new polymer £10 note, due to enter circulation in 2017. She is only the third woman selected to appear on a British banknote. The Jane Austen Literacy Foundation, established in 2014 to provide free literacy resources to communities in need, further honours Jane's enduring appeal. It was founded by Caroline Jane Knight, a fifth great niece of Jane Austen.

What was once the Knight family home in Hampshire now houses the Chawton House Library. Jane would have been very familiar with the house, which once belonged to her brother Edward. Fittingly, the main focus of the library's collections is works written by women between 1600 and 1830. The library holds regular events and exhibitions highlighting the place of women in literature.

Jane Austen and her works have inspired countless books, plays, musicals, film and television dramatisations, and YouTube videos. Some retell her stories; others explore alternative versions through the now popular genre of fan fiction. This diversity is well illustrated by two films released in 2016. The first, *Pride and Prejudice and Zombies*, is based on a quirky piece of fan fiction. The second, *Love and Friendship* starring Kate Beckinsale, is a period drama based on Jane Austen's short epistolary novel, *Lady Susan*.

But ultimately, there would be no Janeites and no Jane Austen industry without her exquisitely written novels. In the words of Sir Walter Scott: 'That young lady had a talent for describing the involvements and feelings and characters of ordinary life, which is to me the most wonderful I ever met with.'[9]

Chapter 10

Rags to Regency Riches – Harriot Mellon (1777–1837)

Coutts bank on the Strand in London, just along from Trafalgar Square, has long been associated with wealth, power and privilege. As a private bank, its services are beyond the reach of most people. Yet during the Regency, this financial establishment for the elite came under the control of a once penniless Irish peasant girl. Her decisions would determine its future.

The story of Harriot Mellon is very much a tale of rags to riches, closely associated with what is still one of the nation's most exclusive financial organisations. But there's more to her legacy than securing the future of Coutts bank. She bequeathed a fortune and a tradition of charity to Angela Burdett-Coutts, one of the most generous philanthropists of the Victorian age.

Early life

The beginning of Harriot Mellon's life was inauspicious. The date and legitimacy of her birth and identity of her father are far from certain. Harriot was born, probably, on 11 November 1777, the daughter of an Irish peasant named Sarah. Her father was, possibly, Lieutenant Matthew Mellon of the Madras Native Infantry, whom Sarah claimed she had married before he returned to India. Lieutenant Mellon reportedly died from consumption on the way to Madras. Either Harriot's father was dead, or a convenient history had been invented to give a degree of respectability to Sarah and her infant daughter. Years later, Harriot's mother claimed that her daughter was of noble blood, if of doubtful legitimacy, but Harriot clung to the more respectable story, that the deceased Lieutenant Mellon was her father.

Eager to escape from the monotony of life as a seamstress, Sarah seized the opportunity of travelling to England with a troupe of touring actors, as their wardrobe manager. With little Harriot in tow, Sarah endured the gruelling life of a strolling player. Soon after, she married a musician, Thomas Entwisle, who was engaged with the troupe. Life for a little girl with a band of strolling players was hard. It involved a lot of walking between towns and sleeping in whatever meagre accommodation her parents could find. Unfortunately, Harriot's stepfather had a fondness for drink, and her mother's volatile temper made life even more difficult. On one occasion, as a punishment, she almost drowned her 4-year-old daughter, and then threw her into a dark shed. Despite this, Sarah had great ambitions for her pretty little girl. She intended Harriot to provide for her financially by catching a rich – and ideally, titled – husband. To this end, she sent Harriot to school whenever she had the opportunity.

It was only a matter of time before Harriot took to the stage. On 16 October 1787, when she was about 9 years old, she appeared as Little Pickle in *The Spoiled Child*, earning 10s. Her mother promptly pocketed the cash and hoped for more. In 1789, the family moved to Stafford where they joined Stanton's theatrical company. Harriot was acting regularly now and her earnings were a guinea, or 21s, a week. John Wright, a Stafford banker, befriended her, and his daughters made a great fuss of Harriot, lending her dresses and jewellery to wear on stage.

Family life was volatile at best. Entwisle's drunkenness meant Harriot had to make excuses for him when he failed to turn up to rehearsals. He also spent money recklessly, causing arguments with Harriot's mother.

Harriot Mellon on stage

In 1794, 16-year-old Harriot seemed on the verge of a step up in her career. Wright introduced Harriot to one of Britain's leading playwrights, Richard Brinsley Sheridan, Member of Parliament for Stafford, who was in town for the races. Importantly, he was also the manager of the Drury Lane Theatre in London. On the basis of Harriot's performance, Sheridan promised to take her on. But the season finished and no offer of work arrived.

Harriot's pushy mother travelled with her family to London to forcibly remind Sheridan of his promise. After three months of nagging, and having enlisted Wright to act on their behalf, Harriot finally got an audition. However, the long-awaited audition was nearly a disaster. Harriot was completely overcome with nerves when asked to read from one of Sheridan's own plays, *The Rivals*. In a flash of inspiration, she asked Sheridan to read the text back to her. This killed her nerves, allowing her to read well, and she left the audition engaged to appear on the stage at the highly respected Theatre Royal, Drury Lane.

Harriot's first appearance was on 17 September 1795 as Lydia Languish in *The Rivals* to reasonably positive reviews.[1] Her performances were never going to compete with the histrionic heights of Mrs Siddons or the comic genius of Mrs Jordan, who were both employed by the Drury Lane theatre at that time. She was given a succession of small parts, and understudied the leading roles, soon earning a reputation for her good nature in stepping in at the last minute to cover the illness of one of the leading ladies before returning, cheerfully, to a minor role. During the summer, when the London theatres were closed, Harriot was engaged to work in Liverpool. Here she played the leading ladies that she had understudied in London. She often returned to Liverpool in subsequent years, sometimes alongside Mrs Siddons. As an attractive, young, single woman, it was hard for Harriot to maintain a respectable reputation on the London stage. Actresses were seen as little better than courtesans and many succumbed to the temptation of becoming the mistress of some wealthy gentleman. As a result, any woman appearing on stage could find herself the target of improper proposals.

Attitudes had begun to change with the arrival of the great actress Mrs Siddons, whose respectability had won her the approval of the royal family. According to Harriot's memoirs, whilst at Liverpool, Mrs Siddons had asked a mutual friend, who often acted with Harriot, how she had behaved in the past. From this report and from what she had observed, Mrs Siddons was satisfied that Harriot was respectable and henceforth showed her considerable kindness, both in Liverpool and in London.

As Harriot was not one of the stars of the London stage, her position remained precarious. She relied on Sheridan re-hiring her at the beginning of each season. Her earnings, though improved, remained slender. Whilst Mrs Siddons made £42 a week in 1802, Harriot took home a meagre £5, but it was an improvement on the £2 she had been earning just a few years before.

A brief romance
During these years on the London stage, there was just one romantic interlude. A Mr Barry, recently arrived from the West Indies, started

paying court to Harriot, and she was in a fair way to returning his affections. Harriot's mother was not impressed. Although this gentleman claimed to have a rich aunt whose property he was set to inherit, he was only a commoner. She still maintained visions of Harriot doing much better for herself.

Harriot's mother did everything she could to thwart the romance, insisting she act as her daughter's chaperone. If playing a third to the couple was not enough, she also pleaded illness in order to cancel their planned outings. She attacked Mr Barry's character and harangued Harriot with accusations of ungratefulness. Harriot confided her distress to one of her friends who, coincidentally, was a family friend of her suitor.

Mr Barry determined to write to Harriot offering her his hand in marriage and claiming he had received a sufficient allowance from his aunt for them to live comfortably. Though unsurprised at the proposal, her friend was quick to point out that Mr Barry had no fortune. Harriot was dismayed to discover that Mr Barry had been lying to her. Had he been truthful, perhaps they would have been married and Harriot Mellon would have sunk into anonymity, a mediocre actress on the Georgian stage, supporting her devoted husband. But Harriot had an abhorrence for dishonesty and could not forgive Mr Barry's deception. She wrote a decisive refusal and never saw him again.

Harriot goes to Cheltenham

Around this time, Harriot's parents moved to Cheltenham where her stepfather set up a music shop, whilst she remained at her house in Little Russell Street with a female companion. When the London season was over, Harriot went to Cheltenham to see her mother. Little did Harriot foresee that her visits would change her life dramatically.

The town's theatre engaged her for five nights and a benefit performance, where she would reap all the profits from the evening's show. Harriot was well received in Cheltenham and her benefit was very successful. So successful, that she yielded to her mother's persuasions to return to the town and see whether a second benefit would give another boost to the family coffers. It did.

In 1805, Harriot took on her most famous role – that of Volante in John Tobin's *The Honey Moon*. Her benefit in the wake of this success was again rewarding, with her admirers sending her generous financial donations in return for a ticket. Through one of these admirers, Harriot managed to secure the position of postmaster in Cheltenham for her stepfather, as some provision for her mother in her old age.

Sarah had a more ambitious plan. She could see that Cheltenham was growing in popularity and persuaded Harriot to invest all her benefit money in constructing a house that could generate a rental income. At first, the returns from the property were very satisfactory, but its success was its downfall. Others copied the idea and as a result of competition, the rental income fell. Sarah urged Harriot to come back to Cheltenham for yet another benefit.

In advance of the benefit, and in her daughter's absence, Sarah worked hard to generate sympathy for their situation. She told how Harriot's plans to provide for her mother had been thwarted by others and that she was performing the benefit to make up for it. As a result, when Harriot later asked for their patronage, few were inclined to refuse.

An elderly admirer
Shortly before the benefit, Thomas Coutts, a massively wealthy businessman who controlled the bank that carried his name, visited Cheltenham for his health. He believed his wife of many years was going mad and had come for a change of scene in an attempt to alleviate his depressed spirits.

On hearing that the old man whom she had spied strolling down the Long Walk was one of the richest people in London, Harriot's mother urged her daughter to write to him. Harriot obediently sent a note inviting him to her benefit performance, but received no reply.

However, a few days after sending her note, as she and a companion enjoyed the Long Walk, Harriot was approached by Coutts himself. The old man apologised for the delay in answering her letter and assured her that he had sent a positive response to the post office that morning. When Harriot got home, she discovered that Coutts had sent five guineas for her benefit – the largest sum of gold that she had ever received from a single person. Harriot put aside the five guineas into a separate purse, declaring that the sum was her 'luck-money' and, despite her mother's pleading, she refused to part with it.

From then onwards, Thomas Coutts took an active interest in Harriot's progress. How much he was encouraged by her mother in the early days, it is hard to tell, but clearly Sarah was delighted with the patronage of such a wealthy man, in whatever form it took. His early letters to Harriot indicate that he looked on her as someone he could support and guide, without any romantic interest.

Coutts admired Harriot's propriety and prudence. Whenever she went out or received visitors she was always accompanied by a female companion. Harriot had always been careful with her money and she was steadily accumulating a bank balance with her bankers, Wright and Co of Covent Garden. Coutts advised her to put her growing fortune into a trust and told her how to ensure that it would remain hers if she married rather than automatically becoming the property of her husband.

Coutts was a curious mixture. On the one hand, he was a hard-headed businessman, the wise, shrewd senior partner in a successful banking enterprise that included the king amongst its customers. On the other hand, he was lonely and depressed, having lost the companionship of his wife of fifty years, who quite probably had a form of dementia. He was desperately in need of distraction and his romantic nature liked to play the 'fairy godmother' in the lives of those less fortunate than himself. Harriot came into his life at just the right time. He was able to be a father figure to her, giving her sound financial advice. He took great pleasure in visiting her as it gave him relief from his depressing situation at home.

Unsurprisingly, conjecture about the nature of their relationship was rife. Because Harriot was an actress, most people assumed that she was Coutts's mistress, though some thought she might be his illegitimate daughter. When Harriot was seen on stage wearing what looked like a diamond necklace, it was rumoured to be an expensive love gift from Coutts. Nobody would believe that it was only costume jewellery bought with her own hard-earned money. She was so upset that she gave the necklace away. On another occasion she won £5,000 from a lottery, but again, it was rumoured that such a large sum must be from her lover.

Coutts gave Harriot presents, but tried to avoid giving her anything that would give rise to speculation and damage her reputation. From November 1805, he paid Harriot an allowance, though he encouraged her not to change to his bank, perhaps hoping to conceal his generosity from his partners and thereby prevent yet more speculation.

Although the relationship was paternalistic to begin with, by the start of the Regency, it was a romance – on Coutts's side at least. During the period 1811 to 1814, he wrote over sixty love letters to Harriot. Although it is possible that Harriot was Coutts's mistress, it seems unlikely that he would have introduced her to his daughters – Susan, Lady Guildford;

136

Frances, Lady Bute; and Sophia, Lady Burdett – if this was the case. Harriot's early biographer, Mrs Cornwell Baron Wilson, was convinced that Harriot's relationship with Coutts was entirely respectable. After Coutts's death, Harriot's reputation was slandered, and she sought legal advice. Wilson wrote that Harriot's legal advisors had examined a wealth of private correspondence and concluded that there was no 'doubt as to the strict propriety of Miss Mellon's conduct'.[2]

The second Mrs Coutts
On 4 January 1815, Thomas Coutts's wife died. Although he was unwell, he made a point of visiting Harriot to give her the news himself. Coutts was aware of his own age and the perilous state of his health and pleaded with Harriot to marry him as a matter of urgency. He wanted to provide for her after his death in the only respectable way that he could. Harriot's first reaction was to refuse, but she was eventually persuaded that if Coutts's health did not improve, she would marry him privately, so that she would have the right of a wife to nurse him if his situation deteriorated.

A fortnight later, Coutts was still very unwell and Harriot agreed to fulfil her promise. As Coutts had recommended to Harriot many years before, the marriage contract gave her full control over the money she brought into the marriage. In addition, Coutts gave her an annuity of £1,000. They were married privately at St Pancras Church on 18 January. They arrived separately, were married by the curate, Mr Champneys, and then they left separately. The ceremony was witnessed by Harriot's friend Mr Raymond, stage manager of the Drury Lane Theatre. Everything went on as before. Harriot called each day to inquire after her husband's health. There was nothing in her behaviour to indicate that she was now his wife. However, some weeks after their wedding, Harriot was given such a dire report of her husband's health that all thought of secrecy was cast aside. Declaring she was Coutts's wife, she took her place at his side, that she might nurse him. Harriot's tender care had its effect and Coutts recovered.

Marriage brought Harriot's career on the London stage to an abrupt end. On 7 February 1815, she performed for the last time. At the end of the play, Harriot went forward and curtsied as Miss Mellon. It was the only indication that she was saying farewell to the stage forever. A month later, on 2 March 1815, *The Times* newspaper announced the marriage of

Thomas Coutts Esq to Miss Harriot Mellon, of Holly Lodge, Highgate. It was cleverly phrased to give the impression the marriage had just taken place, although in reality it had occurred over a month earlier.

Although Coutts had done what he could to prepare his family, reassuring them of his continued affection and future support, the news of his marriage was not received well. Although Coutts's daughters had previously received Harriot with considerable kindness, they now looked on her as a usurper who had conned their father into marriage.

Their behaviour led Coutts to have severe disagreements with two of his daughters, Lady Guildford and Lady Burdett, his nephew, the young Marquis of Bute, and, worst of all, Lady Burdett's husband, the radical politician, Sir Francis. Coutts was very angry and disappointed. He was hurt that his family could not share his pleasure in finding a measure of happiness at his time of life. Presumably the irate family sought proof of the union and, later in March, the entry in the marriage register was declared illegal. No reason was given. Perhaps there was only one witness and the signature of the second witness was added later. Perhaps the door had been locked to ensure privacy thus preventing anyone from being able to declare an impediment to the marriage. We will never know. The couple remarried at St Pancras Church on 12 April and this time there was no doubt as to the legality.

It seems ironic that after all her ambitions for Harriot, Sarah had so little time to appreciate her daughter's new found wealth. Despite all the medical attention that money could buy, Sarah died in May 1815. Harriot had been fiercely loyal to her mother throughout her life, even though she had feared her violent temper and found it hard to escape from her controlling personality. She continued to show kindness to her stepfather for her mother's sake, even though he sank into bad company in the years left to him before he followed her to the grave. After his death, Harriot erected a marble plaque in St Mary's Church, Cheltenham, in memory of her mother and stepfather. Years later, in 1832, she erected a second marble tablet in her mother's honour.

Harriot was devoted to Coutts and referred to him as the best of husbands. They mostly lived at Holly Lodge, a pretty house in Highgate, which she had fallen in love with many years before and had bought with the money she had earned as an actress. Here they entertained, amongst others, the Prince Regent and his brothers, the Dukes of York, Kent and Clarence.

They had seven happy years together before age and infirmity finally caught up with Coutts; he died on 24 February 1822. The funeral was lavish, as befitted such a rich man, and the forty carriages in the procession included those of three royal dukes.

Coutts never forgot the way his family had treated his new wife. In his will, he left his entire fortune to Harriot, including his senior partnership in Coutts bank. He left it for her to decide whether his family should inherit any of his wealth, saying: 'I hope they will all be most kind to her when I am no more, and that my wife may reward them according to their deserts, but not by any means beyond the same.'³ From her humble, almost penniless beginning, Harriot had become one of the wealthiest women in the land.

Life as a widow
After Coutts's death, Harriot became a partner in the bank, now called Coutts and Co, and maintained an active interest in the bank's affairs throughout the rest of her life. She proved to be an excellent banker, regularly scrutinising the books and getting involved in management and investment decisions. Her drawings from the business, which were far in excess of her fellow partners, indicate that she had seniority, despite being a woman.

Unsurprisingly, people tried all sorts of means to get money out of her now that she was such a wealthy woman. Some attempted to blackmail her, threatening to publish unpleasant memoirs of her life, but she was not ashamed of her past and would not be cowed into submission.

She often sought to use her position to do good, although it didn't always succeed. Harriot intervened in the case of a man due to be hanged for trying to pass forged currency at the bank. Her influence saw his sentence commuted from death to transportation, but far from being grateful, his family claimed that it was her duty to pay for them all to emigrate with him and settle them comfortably in New South Wales!

Marriage to the Duke of St Albans
It was at a large dinner party that Harriot first met William Beauclerk, the Duke of St Albans. He was then but 23 years old and known as the Earl of Burford, not yet having come into his title. His father was trying to match him with an heiress, but the young earl was more interested in discussing Shakespeare with Coutts's widow, who was twice his age.

The Beauclerks became part of Harriot's friendship set and in 1825, after the death of his father, the new duke went on a tour of Scotland with Harriot and his sister Charlotte. The duke was enamoured with Harriot, but for a time it seemed that Harriot wanted nothing beyond friendship. They visited Sir Walter Scott at his home at Abbotsford.

Sir Walter could see nothing against the match. If the difference in their ages did not bother them, there was no reason for it to bother anyone else. He wrote: 'If the Duke marries her, he ensures an immense fortune; if she marries him, she has the first rank. If he marries a woman older than himself by twenty years, she marries a man younger in wit by twenty degrees.'[4]

When the duke first proposed to Harriot, she refused, but over time she grew tenderer towards him and when he proposed again, she accepted. The duke was delighted. All he wanted was Harriot, not her wealth. A prenuptial agreement was drawn up allowing Harriot to retain all rights to the disposal of the fortune she had inherited from Coutts. The duke and Harriot were married by special licence on 16 June 1827. Sadly, her second marriage opened Harriot up to a whole new set of abuses. People were more than ready to make up stories about the duchess through jealousy or the hope of earning money.

She loved entertaining, but as she aged, sometimes she was unwell, and the entertainment carried on without her. In one thing she was very particular: she did not like to keep late hours. When she sent out invitations to her balls, she stressed an early start time and got cross if people turned up late. On one occasion, she became so irritated that she ordered the doors to be shut. People were queuing up outside, but not able to get in. When guests started to find entry via the servants' entrance, she laughed, gave in, and reopened the doors. Her anger had passed, but nevertheless, it had been violent whilst it lasted. The duke and Harriot spent many happy times together in Brighton, where they frequently passed the winter at St Albans House. They entertained extravagantly and their hawking parties on the Downs were very popular.

What was Harriot like?
Harriot was a very pretty brunette with a tall, fine figure and a blooming complexion. Although generally good-humoured and pleasant, Harriot had a fierce temper, no doubt inherited from her mother, and was inclined to harbour resentment against those who treated her badly.

She was very superstitious, carrying a book of the prayers of Queen Catherine Parr with her and always avoiding seating thirteen people around the dinner table. Harriot was very sentimental about Coutts's memory and liked to visit his chair in the drawing room at the bank on the anniversary of his death.

Harriot was careful with her money. She made sure she did not get into debt and paid her bills in a timely manner. At the same time, she was very generous. She continued to support her mother and stepfather even when her mother took to scheming in order to get more money out of her daughter. She gave to worthy causes and individuals in need and was always sympathetic to those engaged in the acting profession, particularly comedians. As Duchess of St Albans, she was generous to the poor of Brighton, paying their debts or rent and fulfilling their basic needs directly rather than giving money. She hated dishonesty and became very angry if people sought to take advantage of her generous nature.

Sir Walter wrote of Harriot:

I have always found her a kind, friendly woman, without either affectation or insolence in the display of her wealth and most willing to do good if the means be shown to her. She can be very entertaining too, as she speaks without scruple of her stage life. So much wealth can hardly be enjoyed without the appearance of ostentation.[5]

Harriot's death and will

On her return from Brighton in 1837, Harriot became increasingly unwell. She lost her appetite and was consumed with anxiety. She died in London on 6 August 1837, with the duke beside her. In her will, Harriot left the vast majority of her estate to the Coutts family. She bequeathed Holly Lodge, some other property and an annuity of £10,000 to her husband, provided he did not let either of his brothers or his uncle or their families live with him for as much as a week. Presumably they had not taken the duke's marriage well and had greatly offended Harriot in the process!

Harriot had been very generous to Coutts's daughters during her lifetime and left nothing further to the families of Lady Bute or Lady Guildford. However, she left £20,000 in trust for Lady Burdett, for her 'sole and separate use and benefit, exclusively of any husband',[6] to be divided amongst her daughters on her death.

141

She made a number of small bequests to friends and servants, including an annuity to Eleanor Goddard who had been her companion for almost twenty years, from 1812 to 1831. The remainder of the estate of approximately £1.8 million (worth at least £147.5 million in today's money) was bequeathed, in trust, to Angela Burdett, Lady Burdett's youngest daughter.[7] She had full control of the income, independent of any husband she might have. Angela had been neglected by her mother and often visited Harriot, who enjoyed her company and admired her forceful character.

The will forbade Angela to marry anyone who had not been born British. Incredibly, at the age of 66, Angela broke the terms of the will by marrying her 29-year-old American secretary. By rights, she should have lost all the income of the estate at this point, but she ended up sharing it with the sister who was next in line to receive it. The capital passed to Angela's nephew Francis Money-Coutts, 5th Baron Latymer, on his mother's death.

Harriot's legacy
Harriot had a huge impact on future generations by the way she left her fortune. Coutts left no restrictions on how she disposed of his money and it was her decision to leave the vast majority of it to Coutts's descendants. Harriot chose to leave her enormous wealth to Angela Burdett. One of the conditions of the will was that Angela had to adopt the name Coutts, and as Angela Burdett-Coutts, she is remembered as one of the great philanthropists of the Victorian age.

Thomas Coutts's early biographer, Coleridge, noted that:

> *In the days when George the Fourth was king great wealth, apart from lands and titles, was novel, and its use and disposal were yet to be learned. It was reserved for Miss Burdett Coutts, the inheritor of Harriot Mellon's wealth, to set an example of a wise munificence. But it must not be forgotten that, together with that wealth, she inherited a tradition of charity, perhaps the greater legacy of the two.*[8]

Angela's gifts to the Church of England enabled the building of several churches, including St Stephen in Rochester Row, Westminster, and the purchase of four of the peal of twelve bells of St Paul's Cathedral. She

142

contributed to numerous causes in Britain and overseas, educational, religious and humanitarian, including the RSPCA. In 1871, she was made Baroness Burdett-Coutts in recognition of her charitable work. The Coutts Foundation is a charity established to tackle the causes and consequences of poverty, building on her legacy.

Harriot's will also protected the future of the bank. Her half share was included in the wealth put into trust for Angela, but she was forbidden to get involved in the running of the bank. When the capital was inherited by her son, or, as it turned out, her nephew, he was only to be made a partner if the other partners agreed. Coutts still operates today as the private banking arm of the Royal Bank of Scotland.

Harriot's story is inspirational – a true Cinderella story. In Harriot's own words to Sir Walter Scott after her second marriage:

> *What a strange, eventful life has mine been, from a poor little player-child, with just food and clothes to cover me, dependent on a very precarious profession, without talent or a friend in the world! 'to have seen what I have seen, seeing what I see.' Is it not wonderful? Is it true? Can I believe it? – first the wife of the best, the most perfect being that ever breathed, his love and unbounded confidence in me, his immense fortune so honourably acquired by his own industry, all at my command – and now the wife of a Duke.*[9]

Chapter 11

The Angel of the Prisons –
Elizabeth Fry (1780–1845)

Prisons were grim places in late Georgian Britain. Crime was rising and the system was struggling to cope with increased numbers of inmates. Those awaiting trial were thrown together with hardened criminals awaiting transportation or execution. The result was dirty, crowded institutions, rife with disease and corruption. The situation was worse for women, as they were literally at the mercy of the male staff.

Elizabeth Fry helped to change all this. Starting her prison visiting work with the women of Newgate, she became a major influence on prison reform in the nineteenth century. Less well known is that in 1897, she was acknowledged in the *British Medical Journal* as 'the founder of nursing'.[1]

Struggling through childhood
Elizabeth Gurney was born on 21 May 1780. The following month, the anti-Catholic Gordon Riots all but destroyed Newgate Prison, where Elizabeth's prison ministry later began. Today a plaque commemorates Elizabeth Gurney's birthplace in Gurney Court, Magdalen Street, Norwich, in Norfolk.

She was born into a large family. Her parents, John Gurney and Catherine Bell, both came from families with a strong Quaker heritage. Barred from attending university because he did not belong to the Church of England, John Gurney was unable to enter professions such as the law or the clergy, so he chose to go into business. He became very wealthy and when Elizabeth was 6, he bought a country estate and moved his family out of Norwich to live at nearby Earlham Hall.

Everything was set for Elizabeth to have a happy childhood. And yet poor 'Betsy', as she was called, did not. She struggled with her lessons and her siblings teased her for being stupid. It is highly probable that she was dyslexic, but this wasn't recognised in the eighteenth century.

To make matters worse, Betsy was continually tormented by an excessively nervous disposition. Betsy was afraid of everything. She had nervous headaches and stomach cramps and was often unwell. She was moody and a bit of a loner amongst her siblings. And then, in 1792, her worst fear was realised. Her mother, to whom she had so often clung for protection, died.

Becoming a woman of faith
During her teenage years, Betsy started seeking God in earnest. This caused considerable tension at home as, despite being Quakers, her family disapproved of too much religious enthusiasm.

At that time, Quakers, or members of the Religious Society of Friends, fell into two camps. 'Plain' Quakers were strictly religious while 'gay' Quakers embraced much of what the world had to offer. Betsy's family took the more relaxed approach to their religion. They attended Quaker meetings every week but otherwise they carried on much as any other well-to-do family, wearing fashionable clothes and entering into society.

In 1798, an American Quaker named William Savery spoke at the Goat Lane Meeting House where the Gurneys worshipped. The 17-year-old Betsy was captivated by his words and had a spiritual experience. Betsy was also inspired by the faith of her cousin Priscilla Hannah Gurney, and Deborah Darby, a devout Quaker who had travelled widely as a Quaker minister despite being married and having children. Unlike many other denominations at the time, the Religious Society of Friends commissioned ministers of both sexes. In an age when women had very few rights, it was one of the attractions of the Quakers that they treated men and women equally. Deborah Darby both encouraged and scared Betsy by prophesying over her that she would become: 'A light to the blind; speech to the dumb; and feet to the lame.'[2]

Betsy gradually adopted the ways of a 'plain' Quaker. She assumed the simple Quaker dress and cap and started to address people as 'thee' instead of 'you'. Because of their pagan origins, she stopped referring to days of the week and months of the year by name, and used numbers instead, with Sunday being day one and January month one. In what was a huge wrench, she gave up singing and dancing and visits to the theatre. She admitted in her journal: 'If I could make a rule never to give way to

145

vanity, excitement, or flirting, I do not think I should object to dancing; but it always leads me into some one of these faults.'[3] Betsy committed herself to doing good works. She started a school for local poor children in a disused laundry in Earlham, teaching them herself.

Marriage and a move to London

Betsy had never lacked admirers. At the age of 15, she was engaged to James Lloyd, a member of the Quaker banking family. Betsy suffered an emotional breakdown when it was broken off, presumably by him. Two years later, she was sought in marriage by an officer, but it was not until after her conversion in 1799 that her most persistent suitor appeared on the scene.

Joseph Fry was from an affluent family of 'plain' Quakers. They were not as influential as the Gurneys, but it was considered a good match. When Joseph first proposed, Betsy refused, but eventually she was persuaded to change her mind and the couple married on 19 August 1800. She moved to St Mildred's Court in the City of London to start a new phase of her life.

St Mildred's Court, very close to the Bank of England, was the headquarters for Joseph's business – banking and trading in tea. The couple had little privacy because their home was constantly being used as a base for Quaker activities as well as for people calling on business.

Life in central London was very different to that in the Norwich countryside. St Mildred's Court was on Poultry in Cheapside, home to the Poultry Compter – a small dilapidated prison used to confine debtors and those convicted of crimes such as homosexuality, drunkenness and prostitution. Just a mile away was the notorious Newgate Prison, outside which public executions were held. The overcrowded prison housed both men and women, some awaiting trial, others convicted of crimes that would send them to the gallows or see them transported to Australia.

Betsy ministered to the poor, both from her home and through the Society of Friends who appointed her trustee of a will giving money to the Meeting's poor Quaker widows and a visitor to the Friends' School and Workhouse in Islington.

In 1809, Joseph moved his family out of central London, to his family's estate in Plashet, in what was then semi-rural East Ham. Two years later, as the Regency was beginning, Betsy was appointed a minister for the Religious Society of Friends. She started travelling around the

146

country to speak at different Quaker meetings, often without Joseph, who stayed at home to look after their children. Perhaps it was becoming a Quaker minister, on a par with men, which gave Betsy the courage for the ministry that followed.

Drawing on her experience with the little school she had set up in Earlham before her marriage, Betsy established a school for girls at Plashet. She ministered to local gypsies and during a particularly cold winter, she set up a soup kitchen for the poor. She was also concerned about physical health, becoming a great advocate for inoculation. Through her endeavours, the whole parish was inoculated, practically wiping out smallpox in the area.

Around 1813, Joseph's business started to flounder. Betsy's brothers came to the rescue, but some of the children went to stay with their relatives as Joseph and Betsy were forced to leave Plashet for a while and go back to live at St Mildred's Court in an effort to economise. From this time on, the Frys often moved between Plashet and St Mildred's Court, depending on the financial state of Joseph's business.

Prison ministry
Betsy's first visit to Newgate Prison took place in early 1813. A fellow Quaker had visited the prison and told her about the dreadful state of the female convicts. Betsy decided to see for herself. She visited the prison accompanied by Anna Buxton, the sister of her brother-in-law, the abolitionist Thomas Fowell Buxton. They observed first-hand the pitiful state of the women and their children, who had hardly anything to wear. Betsy's immediate response was to arrange for the naked infants to be clothed.

Perhaps Betsy's prison work would have begun in earnest in 1813 if she had remained in London, but soon she was back at Plashet, dealing with more pregnancies, post-natal depression and the devastating loss of her little daughter, also called Betsy, at the age of 4.

In 1816, the business again faced financial problems, so off the Frys went, back to St Mildred's Court. Betsy had not forgotten the children she had seen in Newgate three years earlier and went back to visit the prison again. The situation had not improved. As a result of an inspection in 1815, the women had been provided with sleeping mats, but the female prisoners of Newgate were still wild and unruly, and deemed to be some of the worst in the country.

Surprisingly, when Betsy spoke, the women listened. There was something in her voice that seemed to have a calming influence on them. Betsy was moved by the plight of the children, locked away with their mothers and having no chance of an education.

It was by their love of their children that she first obtained influence over these abandoned women. When she first took notice of one or two of their fine children, the mothers said that if she could but save their children from the misery they had gone through in vice, they would do anything she bid them.[4]

Betsy had an idea of how she could reshape their future – she planned to establish a school inside the prison. The prison authorities were not very helpful; she was told there was no space and that it would not work. Betsy thought otherwise and the women prisoners also wanted to give it a try. The women agreed to make a cell available for the school and Betsy appointed one of their number to be the teacher. The first prison school in England was established and it soon proved to be a resounding success. Some of the younger convicts begged to be allowed to join the lessons so they too could be educated.

Emboldened by this achievement, Betsy wanted to help reform the lives of the female prisoners as well. She planned to set up a workshop where the women could make things, which they could then sell for a little money to buy articles of clothing and other necessities. She believed this would bring some purpose to the lives of women who had been convicted and were awaiting death or transportation. This project was far more ambitious and no one thought it would work.

Undeterred, Betsy persuaded the prison governor to give his permission for the project, which became known as the Newgate Experiment. She drew up a list of twelve rules, which the inmates unanimously agreed to obey. Behaviour was to be overseen by a matron, supported by a prisoner whose job it was to keep order in the women's yard. The inmates were to be divided into classes and overseen by a monitor appointed from within the group. Cleanliness was encouraged, arguing was discouraged, and swearing was completely forbidden. There was to be no begging, gambling, card playing, plays, novels or immoral songs, whereas attendance at bible readings was compulsory.

In 1817, the Ladies' Association for the Improvement of the Female

Prisoners in Newgate was formed. A matron was duly appointed, funded partly by the local government and partly by the Ladies' Association, and a laundry room became the workroom where the women made stockings for export to Botany Bay. A member of the Ladies' Association visited the prison every day and read passages from the bible to the prisoners. The experiment worked. The atmosphere of the women's side of the prison changed completely. Previously, visitors had noted the restlessness of the prisoners, fighting, swearing and scantily clad. Now there was a sense of calm.

News of Betsy's success spread and she became something of a national celebrity. Other women wanting to set up associations for visiting their local prisons wrote to Betsy for advice. In 1821, The British Ladies' Society for Promoting the Reformation of Female Prisoners became a national society – probably the first national women's organisation in Britain.

Expert advisor on prison reform
In 1818, Betsy had the opportunity to influence the government's policy on prison reform when she gave evidence to a House of Commons Select Committee investigating the state of the prisons. It was the first time that a British parliamentary select committee had ever asked a woman to give evidence.

Betsy described the cramped, dirty conditions in which the women of Newgate lived, and the transformation that had been brought about by her programme of prison visiting, religious education and the creation of the school and workroom. Based on her experience, she made recommendations for the treatment of female prisoners. These included urging the authorities to place women convicts under the care of other women rather than men, who might take advantage of them. She also encouraged the committee to see the advantages of classifying prisoners, separating those who had been convicted from those awaiting trial, and between first time offenders and those who were hardened criminals.

The committee concluded that 'if the principles which govern her [Betsy's] regulations were adopted towards the males, as well as the females, it would be the means of converting a prison into a school of reform'.[5]

Robert Peel's Gaols Act of 1823 incorporated many of the principles that Betsy was advocating, but it did not result in the improvement in prison conditions that might have been expected, because it failed to create an inspectorate to enforce them. In addition, the Act didn't apply to all prisons.

Once the Newgate project was established, Betsy started a programme of visits to other prisons. She travelled with one of her brothers to the north of England and Scotland and later to Ireland. Everywhere she went, she visited prisons, hospitals and lunatic asylums, and spoke at Quaker meetings. Her fame preceded her, but although it gave her opportunities to speak to Queen Charlotte and the Princess of Denmark, it was insufficient to overcome the prejudice of the Roman Catholics in Ireland who hampered her work. Betsy worked frenetically, often only stopping when she reached the point of exhaustion.

In 1827, Betsy published *Observations on the Visiting, Superintendence and Government of Female Prisoners*. As well as giving guidance to Ladies' Associations, it was Betsy's manual for prison reform. She continued to be called upon as an expert witness on prison reform and attended the Select Committee of the House of Lords on the state of all prisons, bridewells and houses of correction in England and Wales in 1835.

The Prison Act of 1835 aimed to bring consistency, with all female convicts being looked after by female officers and the establishment of a proper, paid, prison inspectorate. Although Betsy's work at Newgate was applauded, the general move was away from amateur prison visiting. Perhaps it was this negativism that caused Betsy to publish *Hints on the Advantages and the Duties of Ladies' Committees who Visit Prisons* in 1840.

Betsy was disappointed the government did not want to adopt all her suggestions and she must have questioned the direction of her future ministry. The truth was that the reforms she had helped bring about were now doing much of the work of her prison ministry.

However, Betsy's prison work was far from over. She travelled further afield, visiting prisons in the Channel Islands, Scotland and Ireland, and between 1838 and 1843, she made five trips to Europe, visiting prisons, hospitals and asylums in France, Switzerland, Holland, Belgium, Germany and Denmark. During a visit to Ireland, she was consulted on the first women-only prison being built at Grange Gorman Lane in Dublin and was invited to recommend a suitable person for its first matron, which helped secure its general success.

The plight of the women being transported

Although it is Betsy's work for prison reform for which she is most remembered, her influence was exercised for good in other areas too. This was the time of 'The Bloody Code', where the British legal system had more than 160 crimes that were punishable by the death penalty. These ranged from those you would expect – like murder – to seemingly minor offences in comparison, such as passing a forged bank note. Sometimes the punishment was commuted to transportation, but for the women of Newgate who faced this, it was a terrifying prospect.

When Betsy first became involved in the plight of these women, they were being taken to the ships which would carry them to Australia in open wagons, facing the abuse of passers-by. The women left Newgate with nothing, and the best they could hope for was that they would be hired as a servant on reaching Botany Bay. They faced a high risk of abuse and many were forced into prostitution to survive.

Betsy visited the convict ships and sought to improve the lot of the women who went aboard. Her first success was to have women taken from Newgate in closed carriages, allowing them to maintain some small amount of dignity. Betsy's Ladies' Association provided a bundle of around fifty items for each woman who wanted it to take with her on her journey. The items included clothes and a bible, as well as the materials with which to make patchwork quilts that were in demand in Botany Bay.

If the women behaved well on board, the ship's surgeon could give them a certificate of good behaviour, which gave them a better chance of being hired when they arrived. Where she could, Betsy arranged for missionaries to travel out on the ships, who taught the women to read on the voyage and ministered to their spiritual well-being. The Convict Ship Committee – a sub-committee of The British Ladies' Society – also provided a library of books for each ship.

The women who were not hired as servants were sent to the Parramatta rope making factory. This factory had an appalling reputation and women who went there were particularly open to abuse as no accommodation was provided. Betsy successfully campaigned for a hostel to be built there.

Bankruptcy and disgrace

While his wife was busy reforming British prisons, Joseph Fry's financial problems came to a head and in 1828 he was declared bankrupt. The family was forced to leave Plashet for the last time, moving to a much smaller house in Upton Lane in West Ham. Betsy's brothers were extremely generous, giving her £1,500 a year for her ministry in addition to the £600 salary they paid to Joseph for managing the tea business.

The repercussions of Joseph's bankruptcy were far-reaching. A year after his financial ruin, he was disowned by the Religious Society of Friends, who believed that reneging on your debts was tantamount to dishonesty. The children were angry that their father had been treated so poorly and over time, many of the Fry children left the Quakers for the Church of England. Joseph was eventually reinstated as a member of the Society of Friends in 1838. Betsy felt all the force of her husband's disgrace. She was no longer invited to speak at Quaker meetings. Friends, like William Wilberforce, encouraged her to continue her ministry, but she became depressed and suspended her prison work for a while.

Over the next few years, she met with the Duchess of Gloucester, the Duchess of Kent and her daughter Princess Victoria, the future queen. She concentrated on a new project and in 1831, she published a small book of devotionals, designed to make it easier for people to read the bible. She also led evangelistic meetings in Barking and Dagenham.

The coastguard library project
Soon Betsy had another project to work on. The seeds had been sown years before in 1824 when she was convalescing in Brighton, where she had become aware of the isolation faced by coastguards and their families. These men were not like today's coastguards. Sometimes called blockade men, their primary role was to prevent smuggling. This made them very unpopular with the local community as they posed a threat to a thriving black economy.

Betsy had already provided books for the blockade stations in Brighton and wanted to expand the project. In the 1830s, there were around 4,500 blockade men in Britain manning almost 500 different onshore stations, some of which were extremely remote. This made it very difficult for their children to receive an education. Betsy wanted to provide a library of books for every blockade station. In her usual style, she set up a committee and sought donations to the cause. Perhaps because the blockade men were so unpopular, she found it hard work getting contributions. In 1834, she asked the Chancellor of the Exchequer for a grant of £500 to help the project. Eventually the money was given.

It took two years to complete the project. A list was drawn up of the titles to be purchased and at least fifty-two volumes were delivered to every blockade station in the country. Betsy also ensured that a library was provided at each regional headquarters, so that if a blockade station read all their books, they could borrow more. The government was keen to take credit for Betsy's work and, a few years later, extended the library scheme to the Royal Navy, using the list of books that Betsy had created.

A training school for nurses

On one of her trips to Europe, Betsy visited Theodor Fliedner's training school for nurses at Kaiserworth in Germany. At this time, those who could afford it received what medical attention they needed at home. British hospitals were mostly for the poor and the military, and the calibre of people tending patients was notoriously bad. They were often drunk and immoral. Betsy was inspired by the idea that respectable people could be trained to be nurses to provide care for people in their own homes who could not normally afford nursing services.

In July 1840, Betsy established the Institution for Nursing Sisters at Raven Row, Whitechapel, in London. The nurses' mission was to improve both the spiritual and the physical wellbeing of their patients. The carefully selected women had to be single, either spinsters or widows, of good character, able to read and write, and they had to own a bible. They were given brown print uniforms and caps. Training was, initially, by a three-month placement at nearby hospitals including Guy's, St George's and St Thomas'.

At first the hospitals were sceptical about accepting the trainees, even though they were provided free of charge, but they soon gained a good reputation for helpfulness and eagerness to learn. Once trained, the nurses cared for patients in their own homes at a moderate cost and occasionally free of charge. Sometimes nurses were hired out to hospitals or the wealthy at a commercial rate in order to help fund the Institution. Betsy's health was failing but she was a master at delegation. The nursing project was overseen by her sister-in-law Elizabeth Gurney, with the help of Betsy's daughters.

Although Florence Nightingale is often recognised as being the founder of modern nursing, the credit should really be given to Elizabeth Fry whose nurses were operating in the 1840s, some twenty years before the Nightingale School of Nursing was established at St Thomas'

Hospital. An article in the *British Medical Journal* in 1897 described Betsy as 'the founder of nursing'[1]. Another article published in the same year called her 'the real pioneer of Nursing in this country'.[6]

The Institution for Nursing Sisters continued to operate into the twentieth century, with around 100 nurses at its peak. In 1945, its assets were transferred to the Queen's Nursing Institute, a charity committed to improving patient care in the community.

What was Betsy really like?

Elizabeth Fry was a woman driven by her deep Christian faith and a compassion for those less well off than herself. If she saw a need, she felt a duty to do something about it if she could. She thrived on being busy and worked furiously to achieve her goals, to the detriment of her own mental and physical health, often working to the point of collapse and struggling with depression.

It was not just Betsy's health that suffered; her husband and children suffered too. Betsy was away so often that some Quakers accused her of abandoning her family. Joseph was often left with the children for long periods of time whilst his wife was away and, though he supported her ministry, he sometimes complained that Betsy neglected him. Betsy's marriage was not the Christian partnership that she had hoped for. She was disappointed that Joseph's spiritual commitment was not as deep as hers and, compared to her brothers, she thought Joseph was lazy and incompetent.

Whilst there is no doubt that Betsy loved her husband and children, running a household was not her strong point. She struggled to control her children, whom her sisters unkindly dubbed 'Betsy's brats'. Overwhelmed with feelings of inadequacy, it is hardly surprising that she embraced her ministry outside the home so enthusiastically. Despite her faith, she was plagued with fears throughout her life, especially by a fear of death during her eleven pregnancies.

Her voice has been described as having a captivating musical quality. Maria Edgeworth described it as 'the most sweetly solemn, sedate voice I ever heard'.[7] Yet perhaps the real secret lay in the way she treated people. She showed no favouritism, addressing both princes and prisoners with the same courtesy.

Betsy's illness and death

For years, Betsy struggled against illness and depression only to rally when some need pressed upon her. But finally, on 13 October 1845, Betsy died whilst on holiday in Ramsgate in Kent.

Quaker funerals were typically unpretentious, but Elizabeth Fry's funeral was something different. The funeral procession from her home to the Quaker Burial Ground in Barking was over half a mile long with thirty-nine carriages. Another fifty carriages waited at Barking and over 1,000 people paid tribute at the graveside of this remarkable woman before she was buried on 20 October.

Betsy's legacy

Betsy's prison work was instrumental in bringing about prison reform in the nineteenth century. The evidence that she gave to the House of Commons Select Committee in 1818 convinced them that prisons could be places of reform, not just of punishment – a notion that was far ahead of its time. By encouraging women to visit other women in prison, she was establishing the principle of women working to help other women. She set up the first training school for nurses and ministered to the physical and spiritual needs of countless people.

In 1849, a refuge for female ex-prisoners was established in Hackney in commemoration of Betsy's life. The Elizabeth Fry Refuge was an active, useful memorial designed to continue her life's work. It relocated to Reading in 1962 and continues to operate today as the Elizabeth Fry Charity, providing a hostel for girls on probation.

Amongst the many tributes to Elizabeth Fry is her prominent inclusion at the top of one side of the Reformers' Memorial in Kensal Green Cemetery, erected in 1885. A marble statue of Elizabeth Fry was also erected in the lobby of the Old Bailey in 1914, which stands, appropriately, on the site of Newgate Prison. From 2002 to 2016, Elizabeth Fry was the face on the back of the £5 note. She was only the second woman to be featured on a British banknote, after Florence Nightingale.

Elizabeth Fry's legacy has carried on into the twenty-first century. The difference she made to the women of Newgate has continued to inspire people all over the world. Many of the principles she promoted are embedded in our prison system and penal laws and are still making a difference today.

Chapter 12

The Regency Fossilist –
Mary Anning (1799–1847)

Fossils fascinated people in late Georgian society. This was an age of exciting scientific exploration and these stone bones offered a glimpse into another world populated by giant lizards and strange sea monsters. The notion that many creatures had become extinct in the distant past was a new one. The science of palaeontology – the study of ancient life, largely from fossils – was still in its infancy. Many were keen to collect, and make sense of, these curious relics from the past. But to build a collection required someone to find the fossils, and that in itself was a new skill.

One of the first and most successful fossil hunters of her time was a woman of humble origins from a Dorset seaside town – Mary Anning. Her discoveries made a huge impact on our understanding of the lost world of prehistoric creatures. Despite rarely venturing from her home town and dying relatively young, she's now celebrated as one of the founders of the science of palaeontology.

The girl who lived

Mary Anning's life began right at the end of the eighteenth century, on 21 May 1799. She was born into a very respectable, very ordinary, working class family in the seaside town of Lyme Regis in Dorset. Her parents were Richard Anning, a cabinet maker, and his wife Mary Moore. She should have been one of a large family, but high infant mortality amongst the lowest classes meant illness or accident claimed all Richard and Mary's children except for Mary and her elder brother Joseph.

That Mary made it to her second birthday was nothing short of a miracle. On a hot summer's day in August 1800, an exciting equestrian display was held in Lyme. The show attracted huge crowds of people, including Elizabeth Haskin who had been charged with looking after the infant Mary. Clouds gathered during the afternoon, suggesting that a storm was coming in, but no one wanted to miss the end of the display. Around five o'clock, the heavens opened, scattering the crowds. Most hurried home or took shelter in nearby farm buildings, but Elizabeth and two of her friends unwisely took shelter under some elm trees, along with the young Mary.

The storm was right over the event field. There was a flash of lightning followed by a tremendous clap of thunder. The little group of women under the trees fell to the ground, lifeless. People rushed to the spot, but it was too late. All three women were dead, but somehow the baby had survived. Mary had been turned black, but she was still breathing. She was rushed home to her mother who revived her in a bath of warm water. The blackness wore off and Mary seemed none the worse for the experience.

Unsurprisingly, the story was often repeated and local legend added a magical twist by claiming that after the lightning strike, Mary was transformed from being a dull child into having a lively intelligence! Long before Mary made a name for herself by her fossil collecting, she had gained a local reputation as the girl who lived.

Fossil hunting

Growing up beside the sea, Mary often roamed the beaches and cliffs with her father, Richard Anning, and her brother Joseph. Richard liked to spend his leisure time looking for fossils and there were plenty to be found around Lyme Regis, preserved in the Blue Lias rock and continually being exposed as the sea washed away the cliffs. Today Lyme Regis is part of the Jurassic Coast, a World Heritage site recognised for its important geology, including fossils.

Richard sold his finds – what he called 'curosities' – to visitors as souvenirs, placing them on a table outside their house in Bridge Street. Mary's mother was not impressed by her husband's fossil hunting – carpentry was a much more reliable source of income.

Mary's years of fossil hunting with her father were cut short when she was only 11. One night in 1810, Richard made the mistake of leaving the path and somehow fell over a cliff edge. He survived the fall, but the injuries, combined with the onset of consumption, led to his premature death that winter, at the age of 42.

He left debts behind of £120 – a huge amount of money for a family barely making ends meet. His widow, Mary, and her two surviving children were thrown into abject poverty and faced the prospect of relying on parish relief to keep a roof over their heads. Joseph was apprenticed to an upholsterer and Mary's mother earned a little from lace making, but there seemed little an 11-year-old girl could do to help.

The day after her father was buried, Mary went out walking on the beach. Richard had taught her where to look and, providentially, she picked up a fossil during her ramble. A lady in the street offered to buy the ammonite for half a crown – an offer which Mary eagerly accepted. Mary was delighted. She had discovered a way to help her family survive.

The first ichthyosaur
Mary the fossil hunter began to work in earnest. Accompanied by Joseph whenever he could spare the time from his apprenticeship, she went out looking for fossils to sell. Their first major find was in 1811. They discovered what looked like a crocodile head in an area of cliff known as Black Ven, between Lyme and the next town, Charmouth. Of course, it wasn't the head of a crocodile, it was the head of an ichthyosaur, a huge swimming reptile that had lived more than 100 million years before.

Joseph and Mary retrieved the head, but they had no opportunity to search for the rest of this 'fish lizard'. It wasn't until the following winter that weather and tides allowed Mary to return to Black Ven and locate and extract the ichthyosaur's body. Though not the first such creature ever found, it was more-or-less complete and had been well preserved in the Blue Lias rock. The local paper recorded that they had discovered the fossil of a 17ft long crocodile.

In order to make a living from fossils, Mary needed customers. Fortunately, visiting the seaside had become fashionable in late Georgian Britain, and Lyme Regis, with its distinctive harbour breakwater, the Cobb, attracted its share of visitors coming to bathe in its waters. Only the wealthy could afford to travel, meaning tourists generally had money to spend and Mary could sell them her smaller fossils – mostly ammonites and belemnites – as souvenirs of their stay.

While pocket-sized fossils could be exchanged for a few shillings, major finds like the ichthyosaur were better suited to collectors who were willing to spend a substantial amount of money. There was plenty of interest from individuals and institutions desperate to get their hands on new fossils so that they could increase their knowledge of these ancient creatures. Purchasing a good specimen could bring fame whilst collecting fossils became distinctly fashionable.

Mary's mother soon came round to the notion that finding and selling fossils was a good earner and for the first few years of Mary's fossil hunting, her mother negotiated the sales. Mary was thrilled when she sold that first complete ichthyosaur skeleton to Mr Henley, a local squire, for £23. Henley was keen to put his find on display and passed it to William Bullock's Museum of Natural History in London before it was sold to the British Museum in 1819 for about twice the sum the Annings had received for it. Later it was transferred to the Natural History Museum where the head is still on display today.

This early success spurred Mary into a lifelong fascination with fossils. Although Joseph remained involved in the fossil hunting business until about 1825, his name is not mentioned again in connection with any of the major finds. Mary often went out alone, accompanied by her faithful dog, Tray. It was said that when she discovered a fossil that she wanted to extract, she left Tray guarding it while she went off to hire help to dig the fossil out.

A high profile sale
One of those who came to Lyme looking for fossils was Lieutenant Colonel Thomas Birch, a retired Life Guards' officer. Mary helped him build up his fossil collection. In addition to being a customer, Birch also proved to be a good friend.

Fossil hunting was a financially precarious occupation. It might be months, or even years, between major finds and this left Mary and her family open to periods of financial hardship. Discovering that the Annings were on the verge of selling their furniture in order to pay their rent, Birch decided to sell his collection of fossils to raise money for the near-destitute family of fossil hunters.

The sale took place at Bullock's Egyptian Hall in Piccadilly, London, in May 1820. *The Times* newspaper advertised the sale of a gentleman's small, but fine, private collection of fossils which had been amassed at great expense. No mention was made of Mary Anning, but the advertisement stated that the fossils were 'from the Blue Lias formation at Lyme and Charmouth, in Dorsetshire: consisting principally of bones, illustrating the Osteology of the Ichthio-Saurus, or Proteo-Saurus.'[1] The auction raised more than £400 including £100 for an almost complete ichthyosaur that was sold to the Museum of the Royal College of Surgeons.

Some have speculated that there was a romantic attachment between the 21-year-old Mary and the retired officer, but if there was, it didn't end in marriage. Perhaps it was just on his side or maybe it was more a fatherly interest that Birch took in the young fossil hunter, especially considering that his interest extended to concern for her mother and brother.

More fossil finds
As well as raising money, which helped Mary's family out of its immediate pecuniary difficulties, the sale organised by Birch generated international interest, which raised Mary's profile as a fossil hunter.

It is impossible to say how many significant finds Mary made over the years as she was not always credited with the discovery. More often than not, it was the person who bought the fossil who received the recognition, not the finder. We don't know how many of the fossils found near Lyme that are still on display in museums today were found by Mary. There is plenty of evidence to suggest that she was extremely adept at knowing where to find fossils in the Dorset cliffs.

Selling her finds directly to museums was not always straightforward. In 1821, Mary discovered an almost complete skeleton of a 5ft long ichthyosaur which she hoped that the British Museum would buy. However, they found the price of £100 too high and refused. Instead, the museum chose to purchase an inferior fossil for £50. Even then, they weren't in a hurry to pay up and Mary's mother had to write to the museum to chase payment.

The £100 ichthyosaur was bought by a group of people from Bristol who donated it to the new Bristol Institution for the Advancement of Science in 1823. The ichthyosaur was proclaimed the most valuable specimen in the country, but only the donors' names were recorded – Mary's part was completely forgotten. Bristol writer and fossil collector George Cumberland later put the records straight, acknowledging Mary's role in a letter to a local newspaper, saying that the fossil was due to 'the persevering industry of a young female fossilist of the name of Hanning of Lyme in Dorsetshire and her dangerous employment.'[2] Presumably her name was misspelt because that is how he would have heard it pronounced with a Dorset accent. Unfortunately, this particular

160

ichthyosaur was destroyed when Bristol was bombed during the Second World War. Mary went on to find a number of other ichthyosaur skeletons in the years that followed. The Sedgwick Museum at Cambridge University has used correspondence to confirm that at least six ichthyosaurs in their collection were probably found by her.

Despite her low social class and limited education, Mary made a point of becoming extremely knowledgeable about the fossils that she found. As a girl, she had learned to read and write at the Sunday School of the Congregational Chapel that her family attended, but beyond that, she received no formal education. She taught herself French in order to read the works of George Cuvier, the foremost French anatomist and palaeontologist. She made transcriptions of scientific papers for her own collection, including copying numerous drawings. She dissected modern creatures to compare them to the fossils she found.

Scottish mineralogist Thomas Allan wrote in 1824: 'Mary Anning's knowledge of the subject is quite surprising – she is perfectly acquainted with the anatomy of her subjects.'[3]

Lady Harriet Silvester visited Lyme Regis in 1824 and marvelled at Mary's expertise and the ease with which she conversed with the leading scientists on her subject. Her observations provide some insight into how Mary worked:

> *The extraordinary thing in this young woman is that she has made herself so thoroughly acquainted with the science that the moment she finds any bones she knows to what tribe they belong. She fixes the bones on a frame with cement and then makes drawings and has them engraved.*[4]

A plesiosaur for the Duke of Buckingham
In December 1823, Mary found a virtually perfect plesiosaur – a long-necked sea dragon. British palaeontologists Henry De la Beche and William Conybeare had only recently concluded that the plesiosaur was a different type of fossil from the ichthyosaur. This was the first specimen to be discovered complete with its head and Conybeare rushed to see it, delighted to have his theory proved.

But Frenchman Georges Cuvier was dubious. People had been known to use pieces of fossilised bone from different creatures in order to create a more complete skeleton. Cuvier had seen a drawing of Mary's plesiosaur and, in his view, the fossil was a fake. This was a devastating blow. Cuvier's good opinion was highly regarded by the scientific community. His studies comparing the anatomy of live animals with fossilised creatures had brought him to the conclusion that some fossilised animals had no living counterpart and must, therefore, have died out. The theory of mass extinction was an entirely new idea and led to the emergence of a whole new branch of science to study the fossils of these extinct creatures. As a result, Cuvier has come to be regarded as the founder of the science of palaeontology. Fortunately, a special meeting of the Geological Society concluded that the plesiosaur skeleton was genuine. Cuvier admitted that he had been mistaken and Mary's reputation soared. If he hadn't been persuaded to change his mind, Mary's career as a fossil hunter would probably have been over.

She sold the plesiosaur to Richard Grenville, 1st Duke of Buckingham, for at least £100, possibly more. When Conybeare described the fossil, he failed to mention Mary's role though later she did get credit. When Mary discovered a second complete plesiosaur in 1829, the British Museum bought it for 200 guineas. She sold another one the following year for the same price to William Willoughby, Lord Cole.

A visitor attraction

Mary was becoming something of a tourist attraction in her own right. Her reputation and that of her fossils drew many visitors to Lyme Regis. She was known for being kind and helpful to tourists and scientists alike, although perhaps somewhat eccentric.

Some scientists, however, had little good to say about Mary. Gideon Mantell, a well-known geologist and palaeontologist, was particularly uncomplimentary, describing her as a 'prim, pedantic, vinegar-looking, thin female, shrewd, and rather satirical in conversation.'[5] Others, like Buckland and De la Beche, knew her well enough to appreciate both her uncanny knack of tracking down ichthyosaurs and plesiosaurs in the Blue Lias rock, as well as her scientific insight and knowledge.

In 1824, Mary befriended a young girl, Frances Bell, who had come to Lyme for her health. Frances wrote of Mary: 'She is much noticed by the ladies of the place: and such is her intelligence, that most visitors to Lyme request to be allowed to accompany her in her walks of science.'[6]

One of these visitors was Charlotte Murchison, wife of Sir Roderick Murchison, one of the best known geologists of his time. Charlotte encouraged her husband to take up the science and worked alongside him, but she received little credit for her work. In 1825, Charlotte visited Lyme Regis and, according to her husband, it was here that she learned to become 'a good practical fossilist, by working with the celebrated Mary Anning of that place, and trudging with her (pattens on their feet) along the shore.'[7]

Mary and Charlotte became friends and when Mary made her only known visit to London in July 1829, she stayed with Charlotte.

By 1826, Mary's financial position had improved, and she and her mother were able to move to a house in Broad Street, which provided a better shop for selling fossils. She was still living on Broad Street in 1841 when the census was taken and both she and her mother listed their occupation as 'fossalist'.

The King of Saxony visited Mary in 1844. He wrote:

We fell in with a shop in which the most remarkable petrifactions and fossil remains—the head of an ichthyosaurus, beautiful ammonites, etc—were exhibited in the window. We entered, and found a little shop and adjoining chamber completely filled with fossil productions of the coast.[8]

He continued:

I found in the shop a large slab of blackish clay, in which a perfect ichthyosaurus of at least six feet was embedded. This specimen would have been a great acquisition for many of the cabinets of Natural History on the Continent, and I consider the price demanded 15 sterling as very moderate. I was anxious at all events to write down the address, and the woman who kept the shop, for it was a woman who had devoted herself to this scientific pursuit, with a firm hand wrote her name 'Mary Anning' in my pocket-book, and added, as she returned the book into my hands, 'I am well known throughout the whole of Europe'.[8]

The Philpot sisters and fossil ink
Mary was not the only fossil hunting female living in Lyme Regis at this time, but she was unusual in that she came from a working class background and made her living by selling her discoveries. The three

Philpot sisters were also keen fossil hunters and they often went looking for fossils with Mary. Although they were unmarried, they came from a wealthy family, allowing them to interact with the leading scientific gentlemen of their day as they were of the same social class.

The Philpots, particularly Elizabeth, collected numerous fossils and often lent specimens from their collection to palaeontologists like William Buckland who would study them and describe them for the scientific community, helping them to increase their knowledge.

Around 1828, Mary made a fascinating discovery. She found that a belemnite she was studying had what seemed to be a fossilised chamber containing fossilised ink. With the help of her friend Elizabeth Philpot, she was able to soften the ink and make it useable. There was a nice symmetry in using ink that was millions of years old to draw pictures of fossils which were similarly aged. By dissecting freshly caught squid, Mary came to the conclusion that the belemnite had used ink to defend itself in the same way as its modern-day counterpart.

Pterosaurs, coprolites and other discoveries
In December 1828, Mary found a pterosaur – a winged lizard. It was the first pterodactyl – literally meaning winged finger – to be found outside Germany. Buckland thought the discovery so important that when the British Museum was, surprisingly, uninterested, he bought it himself. When Buckland announced the discovery to the Geological Society of London, he credited Mary with the find. 'Mary Anning … has recently found the skeleton of an unknown species of that most rare and curious of all reptiles, the Pterodactyle.'[9]

Mary was very observant and she noticed that almost every ichthyosaur skeleton she found had a number of stones inside it, near to the ribs or pelvis. She developed a theory that these stones, or bezoars as they were called, were actually the fossilised faeces of the ichthyosaurs. She suggested the idea to Buckland in 1824 and he was sufficiently taken with the theory to investigate further.

Five years later, he presented his findings to the Geological Society, giving full credit to Mary for her help. He named the lumps of fossilised faeces coprolites. It was a more important discovery than it sounds. The analysis of coprolites, some of which contained bones and teeth, helped to bring understanding of the diet enjoyed by these creatures and what the prehistoric ecosystem might have looked like.

In December 1829, Mary discovered a squaloraja – a shark-like creature – most of which was purchased by the Bristol Institution; the tail was part of the Philpot collection and ended up in Oxford.

In 1830, Mary's friend Henry De la Beche illustrated many of Mary's finds in a work of art known as *Duria Antiquior – A More Ancient Dorset*. It included ichthyosaurs, plesiosaurs and pterosaurs interacting together in a busy water scene of 'deep time'. A lithographic print was made from the watercolour and Mary's family received the entire proceeds from the print run.

Fossil hunting was a dangerous business. Mary had to be aware of the tides to avoid getting cut off at the foot of a cliff by the incoming sea, unable to get back to land. She also had to brave the cold of winter as it was the crashing waves of winter storms that often revealed new fossils, making it the best time to go looking. But it was also the time of year when the cliffs were most likely to suffer from landslips. In 1833, Mary wrote to her friend Charlotte Murchison that she had narrowly escaped being crushed to death by a landslip; her poor dog was less fortunate and had been killed.

In 1836, Mary suffered another financial setback. She had trusted an unnamed man with savings of around £200 to invest on her behalf and had been unable to recover them on the man's sudden death. As Mary was usually financially astute, it would seem unlikely that she would have entrusted her money to someone she didn't know without getting a receipt, so either someone tricked her or it was just a very unfortunate turn of events.

Probably due at least in part to the intervention of William Buckland on her behalf, in 1838, Mary was awarded a small pension of £25 a year, financed by the British Association for the Advancement of Science. In addition, a small government grant was procured for her by the prime minister, Lord Melbourne, in return for her contribution to science.

Illness and death

By 1845, Mary was suffering from breast cancer. She resorted to opium and alcohol in an attempt to ease the pain, but unfortunately this led to some malicious gossip that she was addicted to drink. It must have been very upsetting for her in the circumstances. It seems that many of the inhabitants of Lyme didn't appreciate Mary except as a tourist attraction.

The Geological Society raised a subscription to support her in her illness. Around the same time, in July 1846, Mary became the first honorary member of the new Dorset County Museum in Dorchester.

Mary lived all her life in her home town of Lyme Regis and that is where she died, on 9 March 1847 aged 47. She was buried on 15 March at Lyme Regis Parish Church and was posthumously honoured by a commemorative window in the church in 1850.

Mary had a strong Christian faith and was active in church life, both in the Congregational Chapel she had grown up in and later in the parish church. The stained glass window shows pictures of acts of mercy, presumably reflecting the way she helped others. The inscription states that it is in commemoration of Mary Anning's 'usefulness in furthering the science of geology, as also of her benevolence of heart and integrity of life.'[10]

Mary was granted an obituary in the *Quarterly Journal of the Geological Society of London* written by De la Beche – an astonishing honour given that women were barred from membership and the first female Fellow was not elected until 1919!

De la Beche wrote that Mary had 'contributed by her talents and untiring researches in no small degree to our knowledge of the great Enalio-saurians, and other forms of organic life entombed in the vicinity of Lyme Regis' and acknowledged her skill 'in developing the remains, of the many fine skeletons of Ichthyosauri and Plesiosauri, which without her care would never have presented to comparative anatomists in the uninjured form so desirable for their examinations.'[11]

Mary's legacy

Mary Anning was one of the most successful fossil hunters of her time. She had 'a genius for discovering where the Ichthyosauri [lay] imbedded' and 'great judgment in extracting the animals, and infinite skill and manipulation in their development.'[12]

She did not leave behind her a wealth of scientific papers. The only piece of her writing published in a scientific work during her lifetime was an extract from a letter to the *Magazine of Natural History* in 1839 'referring to the supposed frontal spine in the genus Hybodus',[13] a prehistoric shark. Nor did she give her name to any of the fossils she had discovered, although two fossil fish were named in her honour in the 1840s by the Swiss American naturalist, Louis Agassiz, and several more species have been named for her since.

What Mary left us was a wealth of fossils – ichthyosaurs, plesiosaurs and more – many of which are still on display in museums around the world today. Moreover, she made a contribution to the development of palaeontology which cannot be underestimated.

In his *Memoirs on Ichthyosauri and Plesiosauri*, English fossil collector Thomas Hawkins, whose purchases from Mary included a complete 24ft long ichthyosaur, honoured Mary's contribution to the advance of palaeontology. He wrote:

It must never be forgotten how much the exertions of Miss Anning of Lyme, contributed to assist them. This lady, devoting herself to Science, explored the frowning and precipitous cliffs there, when the furious spring-tide conspired with the howling tempest to overthrow them, and rescued from the gaping ocean, sometimes at the peril of her life, the few specimens which originated all the fact and ingenious theories of those persons, whose names must be ever remembered with sentiments of the liveliest gratitude.[14]

Mary Anning was honoured by the Royal Society in 2010 when they chose her as one of the ten most influential female scientists in British history. Most remarkable of all is that she achieved what she did as a single woman without the advantages of class, wealth or education.

To quote the words of Dickens's journal *All Year Round* in 1865: 'Her history shows what humble people may do, if they have just purpose and courage enough, towards promoting the cause of science.'[15]

Notes

Chapter 1 – The King's Stone Maker – Eleanor Coade (1733-1821)

1. *European Magazine*, Volume 41, January 1802, p7.
2. Ibid p8.
3. The obituary in the *Gentleman's Magazine* (see note 4 below) gave the date of Eleanor Coade's death as 18 November 1821.
4. *Gentleman's Magazine*, Volume 91, December 1821, p572.
5. Joe Flood, article on Coade Stone on Coadcoode.blogspot.co.uk (2007).
6. *European Magazine*, Volume 41, January 1802, p8.

Chapter 2 – The Accidental Astronomer – Caroline Herschel (1750-1848)

1. Mrs John Herschel, *Memoir and Correspondence of Caroline Herschel* (John Murray, 1876, London) p6.
2. Ibid p10.
3. Ibid p20.
4. Ibid p218.
5. Ibid p27.
6. Ibid p51.
7. Ibid p52.
8. Ibid p144.
9. Ibid p55.
10. Ibid p64.
11. Ibid p69.
12. *Philosophical Transactions* Volume 77 (Royal Society, 1787, London) p3.
13. Herschel op cit p75-6.
14. Ibid p116.
15. Ibid p117.
16. Ibid p346.
17. Ibid p163.
18. Ibid p216.
19. Ibid p139.

20. Ibid p150-1.
21. Ibid p225.
22. Fanny Burney, *Diary and letters of Madame D'Arblay*, edited by her niece, Charlotte Barrett (Henry Colburn, 1846, London) Vol III p442.
23. Herschel op cit p206.
24. Ibid p182.
25. Ibid p339.
26. Ibid p224.

Chapter 3 – The Upright Actress – Sarah Siddons (1755-1831)

1. The *Oxford Dictionary of National Biography* of Sarah Siddons by Robert Shaughnessy gives her marriage date as the 26 November but Yvonne Ffrench, *Mrs Siddons: Tragic Actress* (R Cobden-Sanderson Ltd, 1936, London) and family history records give the date as 25 November 1773.
2. Thomas Campbell, *Life of Mrs Siddons* (Harper & Brothers, 1834, New York) p33.
3. Ibid p42.
4. James Boaden, *Memoirs of Mrs Siddons: interspersed with anecdotes of authors and actors* (HC Carey & I Lea, and E Littell, 1827, Philadelphia) p229.
5. Ibid p209.
6. Campbell op cit p233.
7. Boaden op cit p141.
8. Ibid p381.
9. Campbell op cit p243.
10. Ibid p244.
11. Boaden op cit p142.

Chapter 4 – Entrepreneur Extraordinaire – Marie Tussaud (1761-1850)

1. *Biographical and descriptive sketches of the whole length composition figures and other works of art forming the unrivalled exhibition of Madame Tussaud* (1823, Bristol) p33.
2. *Biographical and descriptive sketches of the distinguished characters which compose the unrivalled exhibition of Madame Tussaud and Sons* (1842, London) p1.

3. Jehangeer Nowrojee, Nauroji Jahangir and Hirjeebhoy Merwanjee, *Journal of a Residence of Two Years and a Half in Great Britain* (Wm H Allen & Co, 1841, London) p75.

Chapter 5 – The Benevolent Mountaineer – Mary Parminter (1767-1849)
1. The last will and testament of Richard Parminter dated 4 May 1779 with a codicil dated 8 May 1779.
2. *Report and Transactions of the Devonshire Association for the Advancement of Science, Literature and Art* – article by Rev Oswald J Reichel, *Extracts from a Devonshire Lady's notes of travel in France in the Eighteenth Century* (W Brendon and Son, 1902, Plymouth) Vol 34 p269.
3. Ibid p275.
4. Edith Wharton, *Italian villas and their gardens* (The Century Co, 1905, New York) p198.
5. Ibid p197.
6. Ibid p200.
7. *L'Espri des journaux François et étrangers* (Jean-Jacques Tutot, 1786, Paris and Liège) p345.
8. Endowment Deed of the Point in View charity at A la Ronde dated 10 May 1813.
9. Last will and testament of Mary Parminter of A la Ronde near Exmouth dated 11 October 1848.
10. Minutes of the meeting of the trustees of the Point in View charity dated 27 December 1849.

Chapter 6 – Mother of Historical Fiction – Maria Edgeworth (1768-1849)
1. In Maria Edgeworth, *The Life and Letters of Maria Edgeworth,* ed by Augustus JC Hare (Houghton, Mifflin and Company, 1895, Boston and New York), Maria recorded her birth as 1 January 1767. It is now generally accepted that the correct date is 1 January 1768.
2. Richard Lovell and Maria Edgeworth, *Memoirs of Richard Lovell Edgeworth, Esq* (R Hunter, 1821, London) Vol 1 p245.
3. Maria Edgeworth, *The Life and Letters of Maria Edgeworth*, ed by Augustus JC Hare (Houghton, Mifflin and Company, 1895, Boston and New York) Vol 1 p55.

170

4. Ibid p57.

5. Ibid p58-9.

6. Ibid p62.

7. *The British Critic and Quarterly Theological Review* (F & C Rivington, 1800, London) Vol 15 p210.

8. Maria Edgeworth op cit Vol 1 p65.

9. *The British Critic and Quarterly Theological Review* (F & C Rivington, 1800, London) Vol 16 p555.

10. Maria Edgeworth, *Castle Rackrent & The Absentee* (Macmillan and Co, 1903, London) page xxxvi.

11. Margaret Drabble, Jenny Stringer and Daniel Hahn (editors), *The Concise Oxford Companion to English Literature* (Oxford University Press, 2013, online) – entry for *Castle Rackrent.*

12. Maria Edgeworth, *Belinda* (Oxford University Press, 2008) Foreword.

13. Maria Edgeworth, *The Life and Letters of Maria Edgeworth*, ed by Augustus JC Hare (Edward Arnold, 1894, London) Vol 2 p250.

14. Maria Edgeworth, *The Life and Letters of Maria Edgeworth*, ed by Augustus JC Hare (Houghton, Mifflin and Company, 1895, Boston and New York) Vol 1 p112.

15. Ibid p218.

16. Maria Edgeworth, *The Life and Letters of Maria Edgeworth*, ed by Augustus JC Hare (Edward Arnold, 1894, London) Vol 2 p41.

17. Maria Edgeworth, *The Life and Letters of Maria Edgeworth*, ed by Augustus JC Hare (Houghton, Mifflin and Company, 1895, Boston and New York) Vol 1 p219-20.

18. Maria Edgeworth, *The Life and Letters of Maria Edgeworth*, ed by Augustus JC Hare (Edward Arnold, 1894, London) Vol 2 p336.

19. Maria Edgeworth, *The Life and Letters of Maria Edgeworth*, ed by Augustus JC Hare (Houghton, Mifflin and Company, 1895, Boston and New York) Vol 1 p150.

20. Ibid p245.

21. Ibid p286.

22. Maria Edgeworth, *The Life and Letters of Maria Edgeworth*, ed by Augustus JC Hare (Edward Arnold, 1894, London) Vol 2 p35.

23. Maria Edgeworth, *The Life and Letters of Maria Edgeworth*, ed by Augustus JC Hare (Houghton, Mifflin and Company, 1895, Boston and New York) Vol 1 p28.

24. Maria Edgeworth, *The Life and Letters of Maria Edgeworth*, ed by
    Augustus JC Hare (Edward Arnold, 1894, London) Vol 2 p73.
25. Ibid p98.
26. Ibid p267.
27. Ibid p333.
28. Ibid p304.
29. Ibid p332.

Chapter 7 – Faraday's Teacher – Jane Marcet (1769-1858)
1. Jane Marcet, *Conversations on Chemistry,* 5th edition (Longman,
    1817, London) p8-9.
2. Alexander Marcet, *Memoranda*, Volume 4, dated 7 December 1805,
    p 33 as quoted in chapter 2 of *For Better or For Worse?
    Collaborative couples in the sciences* edited by Annette Lykknes,
    Donald L Opitz, Brigitte Van Tiggelen (Birkhauser, 2012) p24.
3. Jane Marcet op cit page v.
4. Thomas P Jones, *New Conversations on Chemistry* (John Grigg,
    1832, Philadelphia) page iii.
5. Dr Bence Jones, *Life and Letters of Faraday* (Longmans, Green and
    Co, 1870, London) Vol 2 p401-2.
6. Ibid Vol 2 p402.
7. Jane Marcet, *Conversations on Political Economy* (Longman, 1816,
    London) Frontispiece.
8. Ibid page v.
9. In a letter to Mrs Ruxton from Maria Edgeworth dated 9 March 1822
    from Maria Edgeworth, *The Life and Letters of Maria Edgeworth*, ed
    by Augustus JC Hare (Edward Arnold, 1894, London) Vol 2 p65.
10. Jane Marcet, *Conversations on Political Economy* (Longman, 1816,
    London) pages vi-vii.
11. Ibid p11-12.
12. Harriet Martineau, *Biographical sketches* (Leypoldt & Holt, 1869,
    New York) p72-3.
13. Ibid p75.
14. In a letter from Maria Edgeworth dated Sept 1820 from Maria
    Edgeworth, *The Life and Letters of Maria Edgeworth*, ed by
    Augustus JC Hare (Edward Arnold, 1894, London) Vol 2 p14.
15. *The Edinburgh Annual Register for 1822* Volume 15 (Archibald
    Constable & Co, 1824, Edinburgh) p398.

NOTES

16. Jane Marcet, *Conversations on the Evidences of Christianity* (Longman, 1826, London) page iv.
17. Martineau op cit p73.
18. *The Literary Gazette and Journal of Belles Lettres, Arts, Sciences, & c* (WA Scripps, 1845, London) p343.
19. Martineau op cit p75.
20. Ibid p72.

Chapter 8 – Engineering Enthusiast – Sarah Guppy (1770-1852)
1. The relative values of these sums of money from 1804 compared with 2015 were computed using the calculators on the MeasuringWorth.com website.
2. The *Monthly Review or Literary Journal* (R Griffiths, 1801, London) Vol 34 p202.
3. Charmian Barker, *A Vigorous Bristol Family* (Unpublished research, 1995, accessed 1 April 2016 at Bristol Records Office) – a letter by Sarah Guppy to Arthur Young dated March 1811.
4. Ibid – a letter from Sarah Guppy to 2nd Earl of Liverpool dated July 1811 in British Library – transcription from Liverpool Papers, Vol LXVII Add 38 246 f178.
5. *The Repertory of Arts, Manufactures and Agriculture* 2nd series (J Wyatt, 1811, London) Volume 19 p215.
6. Madge Dresser, *Sarah Guppy [née Beach, other married name Coote], (1770-1852), Oxford Dictionary of National Biography* (Oxford University Press, April 2016; accessed 19 Jun 2016).
7. *The Mechanics' Magazine* (ed RA Brooman and EJ Reed) (Robertson, Brooman & Co, 1860, London) p76.
8. *The Repertory of Arts, Manufactures and Agriculture* 2nd series (J Wyatt, 1812, London) Vol 21 p142.
9. Ibid p144.
10. Barker op cit, will of Samuel Guppy dated 16 May 1817.
11. *The Repertory of Patent Inventions and other Discoveries and Improvements in Arts, Manufactures and Agriculture* (1832) Vol 13 p338.
12. Barker op cit – quote from Sarah's great granddaughter Theodora Cayley Robinson in 1926.
13. Barker op cit - Obituary in Bristol Mercury and Western Counties Advertisement 28 August 1852.

14. Barker op cit - Obituary of Thomas Richard Guppy in Bristol Mercury and Daily Post 8 July 1882.

Chapter 9 – Mr Darcy's Maker – Jane Austen (1775-1817)

1. William and Richard Arthur Austen-Leigh, *Jane Austen, Her Life and Letters* (Smith, Elder & Co, 1913, London) p87 - in a letter to Cassandra dated 9 January 1796.
2. Jane Austen, *Pride and Prejudice* (Thomas Egerton, 1813, London) Chapter 3.
3. Ibid Chapter 34.
4. Jane Austen, *Sense and Sensibility* (Thomas Egerton, 1811, London) – frontispiece.
5. Jane Austen, *Pride and Prejudice* (Thomas Egerton, 1813, London) – frontispiece.
6. Jane Austen, *Emma* (John Murray, 1815, London) Chapter 10.
7. Jane Austen, *Persuasion* (John Murray, 1817, London) Chapter 23.
8. James Edward Austen-Leigh, *A Memoir of Jane Austen* (Richard Bentley and Son, 1871, London) p87.
9. Sir Walter Scott, *The Journal of Sir Walter Scott: from the original manuscript at Abbotsford* (David Douglas, 1891, Edinburgh) p155 – entry for 14 March 1826.

Chapter 10 – Rags to Regency Riches – Harriot Mellon (1777-1837)

1. The date of Harriot's first performance in London was given as 17 September 1795 in Mrs Cornwell Baron Wilson's, *Memoirs of Miss Mellon, afterwards Duchess of St Albans*, Vol 1 (Remington and Co, 1886, London) p149. A much earlier date of 31 January 1795 was given by Joan Perkin in the entry for *Harriot Beauclerk, duchess of St Albans (1777?-1837) Oxford Dictionary of National Biography* (Oxford University Press, 2004; online edn Jan 2008, accessed 24 Aug 2015).
2. Mrs Cornwell Baron Wilson, *Memoirs of Miss Mellon, afterwards Duchess of St Albans*, Vol 1 (Remington and Co, 1886, London) p15.
3. In a letter from Thomas Coutts to his solicitor, John Parkinson, dated 3 May 1820 in Ernest Hartley Coleridge, *The Life of Thomas Coutts Banker* (John Lane, 1920, London) Vol 2, p369.
4. Sir Walter Scott, *The Journal of Sir Walter Scott: from the original manuscript at Abbotsford* (David Douglas, 1891, Edinburgh) Vol 1 p19.

5. Ibid p18-19.
6. From the official copy of the will of the Duchess of St Albans extracted from the Registry of the Prerogative Court of Canterbury in Mrs Cornwell Baron-Wilson, *Memoirs of Harriot, Duchess of St Albans*, 2nd edition (Henry Colburn, 1840, London) Vol 2 p329.
7. The relative value of Harriot's estate in 1837 in today's money was computed using the calculators on the MeasuringWorth.com website.
8. Coleridge op cit p248.
9. Scott op cit p414 - in a letter from Harriot, Duchess of St Albans in reply to Sir Walter Scott's letter of congratulation on her marriage, dated 16 July 1827.

Chapter 11 – The Angel of the Prisons – Elizabeth Fry (1780-1845)
1. RG Huntsman, Mary Bruin, Mary and Deborah Holttum, *Twixt candle and lamp: the contribution of Elizabeth Fry and the Institution of Nursing Sisters to Nursing Reform, Medical History* (2012) Vol 46, p351 – quoting an editorial, *"The nursing of the sick under Queen Victoria" British Medical Journal* 1897, 1644-8, p1645.
2. Susanna Corder, *Life of Elizabeth Fry: Compiled from her journal, as edited by her daughters, and from various other sources* (Henry Longstreth, 1853, Philadelphia) p62.
3. Ibid p70.
4. Maria Edgeworth, *The Life and Letters of Maria Edgeworth*, ed by Augustus JC Hare (Edward Arnold, 1894, London) Vol 2 p69.
5. Sylvanus Urban, *The Gentleman's Magazine* (John Bowyer Nichols and Son, 1845, London) Vol 24, p644-5 - Report of Grand Jury of London in February 1818 as reported in Betsy's obituary.
6. Huntsman, Bruin and Holttum op cit p351 – quoting an article, *Nursing in the Victorian era* by Margaret Breay in *Nursing Record and Hospital Wold* 1897.
7. Edgeworth op cit p68.

Chapter 12 – The Regency Fossilist – Mary Anning (1799-1847)
1. 'Sales by Auction.' *Times* (London, England, 10 May 1820: 4. *The Times Digital Archive*. Web. 24 June 2016.
2. Larry E Davis, *Mary Anning: Princess of Palaeontology and Geological Lioness, The Compass: Earth Science Journal of Sigma Gamma Epsilon* (2012) Vol 84: Iss 1, Article 8 p74.

3. Ibid p68.
4. *Mary Anning* article on The Geological Society website.
5. Davis op cit p66.
6. Rev Johnson Grant, *A Memoir of Miss Frances Augusta Bell* (Hatchard & Son, 1827, London) Frances Bell letter 1824 p121.
7. Archibald Geikie, *Life of Sir Roderick I Murchison* (John Murray, 1875, London) Vol 2 p334.
8. Mrs Gordon, *The Life and Correspondence of William Buckland, DD, FRS* (John Murray, 1894, London) p115.
9. Davis op cit p76.
10. Gordon op cit p116.
11. Davis op cit p68-9.
12. George Roberts, *The History and Antiquities of the borough of Lyme Regis and Charmouth* (Samuel Bagster, 1834, London) p290.
13. *The magazine of natural history and journal of zoology, botany, mineralogy, geology and meteorology* (Longman, 1839, London) p605.
14. Thomas Hawkins, *Memoirs of Ichthyosauri and Plesiosauri, Extinct Monsters of the Ancient Earth* (Rolfe and Fletcher, 1834, London) p9.
15. *All Year Round* - A weekly journal conducted by Charles Dickens (1865, London) Vol 13 p63.

List of Illustrations

1. King's Statue, Weymouth seafront, Weymouth, Dorset. A Coade stone memorial erected in 1809 to celebrate George III's jubilee. Photograph © Andrew Knowles.
2. The entrance to Coade and Sealy's Gallery of Sculpture of Artificial Stone, Westminster Bridge from *The European Magazine and London Review* Vol 41 (1802).
3. William Herschel's telescope from *L'Espace céleste et la nature tropicale, description physique de l'univers* ... by Emmanuel Liais (1866).
4. Drury Lane Theatre from the stage during a performance, a copper plate by Richard Phillips, from *Modern London; being the history and present state of the British Metropolis* (1804).
5. Mrs Siddons as the Tragic Muse by Sir Joshua Reynolds from *How to study pictures* ... by Charles Henry Caffin (1910).
6. Madame Tussaud from *Old and New London: A narrative of its history, its people, and its places* by Edward Walford Vol 4 (1873).
7. A la Ronde, Exmouth, Devon. With kind permission of the National Trust. Photograph © Andrew Knowles.
8. Maria Edgeworth from *Crowned masterpieces of literature that have advanced civilization, as preserved and presented by the world's best essays, from the earliest period to the present time* by David J Brewer, Edward A Allen and William Schuyler (1908).
9. The Royal Institution, Albemarle Street, London, from *Old and New London: A narrative of its history, its people, and its places* by Edward Walford Vol 4 (1873).
10. An illustration from *Conversations on Chemistry* by Jane Marcet, 5th edition, Vol 1 (1817).
11. Clifton Suspension Bridge from *Industrial rivers of the United Kingdom ... By various well-known experts, etc* [Edited by Evan Rowland Jones. Reprinted from the *Shipping World*.] (1888).
12. Chawton Cottage, now Jane Austen's House Museum, Chawton, near Alton, Hampshire. Photograph © Andrew Knowles.

13. Jane Austen Festival 2014 Regency Promenade in Bath. Photograph © Andrew Knowles.
14. Harriot Coutts (née Mellon) from *The Life of Thomas Coutts Banker* by Ernest Hartley Coleridge Vol 2 (1920).
15. Elizabeth Fry visits Newgate Prison from *Some famous women* by Louise Creighton (1909).
16. Fossils on the beach at Lyme Regis, Dorset. Photograph © Andrew Knowles.

Additional picture used in cover design: Plate 18 – Promenade Costumes – from *The Repository of Arts, Literature, Commerce, Manufactures, Fashions, and Politics* for September 1810 published by Rudolph Ackermann.

Select Bibliography

All Year Round - A weekly journal conducted by Charles Dickens (1865, London) Vol 13

Austen, Jane, *Emma* (John Murray, 1815, London)

Austen, Jane, *My dear Cassandra, letters to her sister* selected and introduced by Penelope Hughes-Hallett (Collins & Brown Ltd, 1990, London)

Austen, Jane, *Northanger Abbey and Persuasion* (John Murray, 1817, London)

Austen, Jane, *Pride and Prejudice* (Thomas Egerton, 1813, London)

Austen, Jane, *Sense and Sensibility* (Thomas Egerton, 1811, London)

Austen, Jane, *The Letters of Jane Austen selected from the compilation of her great nephew, Edward, Lord Bradbourne* ed Sarah Woolsey (Little, Brown, and Co, 1908, Boston)

Austen-Leigh, James Edward, *A Memoir of Jane Austen* (Richard Bentley and Son, 1871, London)

Austen-Leigh, William and Richard Arthur, *Jane Austen, Her Life and Letters* (Smith, Elder & Co, 1913, London)

Bagshaw, Kaye, *Parminter, Jane (1750-1811), Oxford Dictionary of National Biography* (Oxford University Press, 2004; online edn Sept 2014, accessed 19 Sept 2015)

Barker, Charmian, *A Vigorous Bristol Family* (Unpublished research, 1995, accessed 1 April 2016 at Bristol Records Office)

Bell, John, *La Belle Assemblée* (John Bell, 1812, London)

Berridge, Kate, *Madame Tussaud, A Life in Wax* (Harper Perennial, 2007)

Biographical and descriptive sketches of the distinguished characters which compose the unrivalled exhibition of Madame Tussaud and Sons (1842, London)

Biographical and descriptive sketches of the whole length composition figures and other works of art forming the unrivalled exhibition of Madame Tussaud (1823, Bristol)

Boaden, James, *Memoirs of Mrs Siddons: interspersed with anecdotes of authors and actors* (HC Carey & I Lea, and E Littell, 1827, Philadelphia)

Brooman, RA and Reed, EJ (Ed) *The Mechanics' Magazine* Vol 3 (Jan to June 1860)

Burney, Fanny, *Diary and letters of Madame D'Arblay*, edited by her niece, Charlotte Barrett (Henry Colburn, 1846, London) Vol III

Butler, Marilyn, *Austen, Jane (1775-1817), Oxford Dictionary of National Biography* (Oxford University Press, 2004; online edn Jan 2010, accessed 2 July 2013)

Campbell, Thomas, *Life of Mrs Siddons* (Harper & Brothers, 1834, New York)

Cecil, David, *A Portrait of Jane Austen* (Constable, 1978; Penguin, 1980, London)

Coleridge, Ernest Hartley, *The Life of Thomas Coutts Banker* (John Lane, 1920, London)

Coley, NG, *Marcet, Alexander John Gaspard (1770-1822), Oxford Dictionary of National Biography* (Oxford University Press, 2004; accessed 6 June 2016)

Concannon, Undine, *Tussaud, Anna Maria (bap 1761, d 1850) Oxford Dictionary of National Biography* (Oxford University Press, 2004; accessed 24 Aug 2015)

Corder, Susanna, *Life of Elizabeth Fry: Compiled from her journal, as edited by her daughters, and from various other sources* (Henry Longstreth, 1853, Philadelphia)

Curle, Richard, *Mary Anning (1799-1847),* Dorset Worthies no.4 (1963)

Davis, Larry E, *Mary Anning: Princess of Palaeontology and Geological Lioness, The Compass: Earth Science Journal of Sigma Gamma Epsilon* (2012) Vol 84: Iss 1, Article 8

Dawes, Margaret and Selwyn, Nesta, *Women who made money - women partners in British private banks 1752-1906* (Trafford Publishing, USA, 2010)

De Haan, Franciscas, *Fry (née Gurney) Elizabeth (1780-1845), Oxford Dictionary of National Biography* (Oxford University Press, 2004; online edn May 2007, accessed 24 Aug 2015)

Drabble, Margaret, Stringer, Jenny and Hahn, Daniel, *The Concise Oxford Companion to English Literature* (Oxford University Press, 2013, online)

Draper, Jo, *Mary Anning and me*, article in *Dorset Life – The Dorset Magazine* online (2010)

Dresser, Madge, *Guppy [née Beach, other married name Coote], Sarah (1770-1852), Oxford Dictionary of National Biography* (Oxford University Press, April 2016; accessed 19 Jun 2016)

Edgeworth, Maria and Richard Lovell, *Practical Education* (J Johnson, 1798, London)

Edgeworth, Maria, *Belinda* (Oxford University Press, 2008)

Edgeworth, Maria, *Castle Rackrent & The Absentee* (Macmillan and Co, 1903, London)

Edgeworth, Maria, *Letters for Literary Ladies* (J Johnson, 1795, London)

Edgeworth, Maria, *The Life and Letters of Maria Edgeworth*, ed by Augustus JC Hare (Edward Arnold, 1894, London) Vol 2

Edgeworth, Maria, *The Life and Letters of Maria Edgeworth*, ed by Augustus JC Hare (Houghton, Mifflin and Company, 1895, Boston and New York) Vol 1

Edgeworth, Richard Lovell and Maria, *Memoirs of Richard Lovell Edgeworth esq* (R Hunter, 1821, London)

Emling, Shelley, *The Fossil Hunter* (Palgrave Macmillan, 2009, New York)

Ffrench, Yvonne, *Mrs Siddons: Tragic Actress* (R Cobden-Sanderson Ltd, 1936, London)

Flood, Joe, *Coade Stone* (Coadcoode.blogspot.co.uk, 2007)

Fry, Elizabeth, *Observations on the visiting, superintendence, and government, of female prisoners* (John and Arthur Arch, 1827, London)

Geikie, Archibald, *Life of Sir Roderick I Murchison* (John Murray, 1875, London)

Gordon, Mrs, *The Life and Correspondence of William Buckland, DD, FRS* (John Murray, 1894, London)

Grant, Rev Johnson, *A Memoir of Miss Frances Augusta Bell* (Hatchard & Son, 1827, London)

Graves, Algernon, *The Society of Artists of Great Britain, 1760-1791, the Free Society of Artists, 1761-1783: a complete dictionary of contributors and their work* (George Bell and Sons, 1907, London)

Harding, Lt Col, *The History of Tiverton, in the County of Devon: book 1* (F Boyce, 1845, Tiverton)

Hatton, Jean, *Betsy – The dramatic biography of prison reformer Elizabeth Fry* (Monarch Books, 2005, Oxford)

Hawkins, Thomas, *Memoirs of Ichthyosauri and plesiosauri, Extinct Monsters of the Ancient Earth* (Rolfe and Fletcher, 1834, London)

Herschel, Mrs John, *Memoir and Correspondence of Caroline Herschel* (John Murray, 1876, London)

Hoskin, Michael, *Herschel, Caroline Lucretia (1750-1848), Oxford Dictionary of National Biography* (Oxford University Press, 2004; online edn Oct 2005, accessed 24 Aug 2015)

Hoskin, Michael, *Herschel, William (1738-1822), Oxford Dictionary of National Biography* (Oxford University Press, 2004; online edn Oct 2008, accessed 22 June 2016)

Huntsman, RG, Bruin, Mary and Holttum, Deborah, *Twixt candle and lamp: the contribution of Elizabeth Fry and the Institution of Nursing Sisters to Nursing Reform, Medical History* (2012) Vol 46, p351-380

Isba, Anne, *The Excellent Mrs Fry - Unlikely Heroine* (Continuum International Publishing Group, 2010, New York)

James, Frank AJL, *Guides to the Royal Institution of Great Britain: 1 History* (Royal Institution of Great Britain, 2000)

Jones, Dr Bence, *Life and Letters of Faraday* (Longmans, Green and Co, 1870, London)

Jones, Thomas P, *New Conversations on Chemistry* (John Grigg, 1832, Philadelphia)

Kelly, Alison, *Coade, Eleanor (1733-1821) Oxford Dictionary of National Biography* (Oxford University Press, 2004, online edition accessed 24 Aug 2015)

Kelly, Alison, *Mrs Coade's Stone* (Self Publishing Association, 1990)

L'Espri des journaux François et étrangers Vol 12 (Jean-Jacques Tutot, 1786, Paris and Liège)

Lykknes, Annette, Opitz, Donald L, Van Tiggelen, Brigitte (Editors), *For Better or For Worse? Collaborative couples in the sciences* (Birkhauser, 2012)

Marcet, Jane, *Conversations on Political Economy* (Longman, 1816, London)

Marcet, Jane, *Conversations on the Evidences of Christianity* (Longman, 1826, London)

Marcet, Mrs, *Conversations on Chemistry* 5th edition (Longman, 1817, London)

Marcet, Mrs, *Conversations on Natural Philosophy* 13th edition (Longman, 1858, London)

Martineau, Harriet, *Biographical sketches* (Leypoldt & Holt, 1869, New York)

McCormack, WJ, *Edgeworth, Maria (1768-1849), Oxford Dictionary of National Biography* (Oxford University Press, 2004; online edn Jan 2008, accessed 24 Aug 2015)

Meller, Hugh, *A La Ronde, National Trust guidebook* (National Trust, 1993, this edition 2004)

Morse, Elizabeth J, *Marcet, Jane Haldimand (1769-1858), Oxford Dictionary of National Biography* (Oxford University Press, 2004; accessed 24 Aug 2015)

National Trust, *The Story of A La Ronde and its People* (National Trust, 2011, revised 2013, accessed online 27 August 2015)

Newton, William, *The London journal of arts and sciences* Vol 25 (W Newton, 1844, London)

Newton, William, *The London journal of arts and sciences* Vol 8 (Sherwood, Gilbert and Piper, 1832, London)

Nowrojee, Jehangeer, Jahangir, Nauroji and Merwanjee, Hirjeebhoy, *Journal of a Residence of Two Years and a Half in Great Britain* (Wm H Allen & Co, 1841, London)

Perkin, Joan, *Beauclerk, Harriot, duchess of St Albans (1777?-1837) Oxford Dictionary of National Biography* (Oxford University Press, 2004; online edn Jan 2008, accessed 24 Aug 2015)

Philosophical Transactions (Royal Society, 1787, London) Vol 77

Pilbeam, Pamela, *Madame Tussaud and the history of waxworks* (Hambledon and London, 2003)

Pritchard, Andrew, *English patents* (Whittaker and Co, 1847, London)

Reichel, Rev Oswald J, *Extracts from a Devonshire Lady's notes of travel in France in the Eighteenth Century in Report and Transactions of the Devonshire Association for the Advancement of Science, Literature and Art* Vol 34, p265-275 (W Brendon and Son, 1902, Plymouth)

Richards, Laura E, *Elizabeth Fry, The Angel of the Prisons* (D Appleton and Co, 1916, New York)

Roberts, George, *The History and Antiquities of the borough of Lyme Regis and Charmouth* (Samuel Bagster, 1834, London)

Roberts, Sir Howard and Godfrey, Walter H (editors), *Survey of London Volume XXIII - South Bank & Vauxhall Part 1* (London County Council, 1951, London)

Robinson, John Martin, *Buckingham Palace, The official illustrated history* (Royal Collections Enterprises Ltd, 2011)
Scott, Sir Walter, *The Journal of Sir Walter Scott: from the original manuscript at Abbotsford* (David Douglas, 1891, Edinburgh)
Shaughnessy, Robert, *Siddons, Sarah (1755-1831), Oxford Dictionary of National Biography* (Oxford University Press, 2004, online edn May 2008, accessed 11 Feb 2013)
Shepherd, FHW, *Survey of London* (1963, British History online, accessed 7 February 2013)
The British Critic and Quarterly Theological Review (F & C Rivington, 1800, London)
The Edinburgh Annual Register for 1822 (Archibald Constable & Co, 1824, Edinburgh)
The European Magazine and London Review Vol 11 (1787)
The European Magazine and London Review Vol 41 (1802)
The Literary Gazette and Journal of Belles Lettres, Arts, Sciences, & c (WA Scripps, 1845, London)
The magazine of natural history and journal of zoology, botany, mineralogy, geology and meteorology (Longman, 1839, London)
The Monthly Review or Literary Journal Vol 34 (R Griffiths, 1801, London)
The Repertory of Arts, Manufactures and Agriculture Vol 19 2nd series (J Wyatt, 1811, London)
The Repertory of Arts, Manufactures and Agriculture Vol 21 2nd series (J Wyatt, 1812, London)
The Repertory of Patent Inventions and other Discoveries and Improvements in Arts, Manufactures and Agriculture Vol 1 (1832)
The Times Digital Archive
Tilloch, Alexander and Taylor, Richard, *Philosophical Magazine* Vol 64 (1824, London)
Tilloch, Alexander, *Philosophical Magazine* Vol 20 (1805, London)
Tilloch, Alexander, *Philosophical Magazine* Vol 37 (1811, London)
Tilloch, Alexander, *Philosophical Magazine* Vol 38 (1811, London)
Tilloch, Alexander, *Philosophical Magazine* Vol 39 (1812, London)
Torrens, HS, *Anning, Mary (1799-1847) Oxford Dictionary of National Biography* (Oxford University Press, 2004; online edn Jan 2008, accessed 5 Oct 2012)

SELECT BIBLIOGRAPHY

Torrens, Hugh, *Mary Anning (1799-1847) of Lyme, 'the greatest fossilist the world ever knew'. British Journal for History of Science*, 28, pp257-284

Tussaud, Madame, *Madame Tussaud's Memoirs and Reminiscences of France, forming an abridged history of the French Revolution*, ed F Hervé (Saunders and Otley, 1838, London)

Urban, Sylvanus, *The Gentleman's Magazine* Vol 24 (John Bowyer Nichols and Son, 1845, London)

Urban, Sylvanus, *The Gentleman's Magazine* Vol 91 (John Nichols and Son, 1821, London)

Walford, Edward, *Old and New London: A narrative of its history, its people, and its places* (Cassell, Petter & Galpin, 1873, London) Vol 4

Wharton, Edith, *Italian villas and their gardens* (The Century Co, 1905, New York)

Wilson, Mrs Cornwell Baron, *Memoirs of Harriot, Duchess of St Albans* 2nd edition Vol 2 (Henry Colburn, 1840, London)

Wilson, Mrs Cornwell Baron, *Memoirs of Miss Mellon, afterwards Duchess of St Albans* Vol 1 (Remington and Co, 1886, London)

Index

A la Ronde, Exmouth, 10, 13, 66, 73-4, 75-7
Absentee, The, 85
Aikin, Arthur, 96
Alfred, King, 22
Almack's Assembly Rooms, 88
Almshouses, 74, 76
Alps, 13, 71
Amelia, Princess, 7, 36
Amiens, Peace of, 59, 86,
Animal welfare, 109-10, 143
Anning, Mary:
  birth and early years, 156-8
  character and appearance, 162, 163, 166
  Christian faith, 166
  education, 11, 161
  financial problems, 158, 159-60, 165, 166
  fossil hunter, 157-65
  friendship with:
    Bell, Frances, 162
    Birch, Lieutenant Colonel Thomas, 159-60
    Buckland, William 162, 165
    De la Beche, Henry, 162, 165
    Murchison, Charlotte, 162-3
    Philpot sisters, 163-4
  honoured, 14, 165, 166, 167
  illness and death, 165-6
  legacy, 166-7
  lightning strike, 156-7
  relationship with mother, 159, 160, 163

Argyll Rooms, 51
Astronomer Royal, 32, 33
Astronomical Society, *see* Royal Astronomical Society (previously Astronomical Society)
Astronomy, 28, 29, 31-40
Atlas Coelestis, 33
Aubert, Alexander, 34
Augusta, Princess, 36
Austen, Anna, 123
Austen, Cassandra (Jane Austen's sister):
  artist, 119, 128
  education, 118
  engagement, 120, 126
  relationship with sister, Jane, 118, 119, 121, 122-3
Austen, Cassandra (previously Leigh, Jane Austen's mother), 117, 121, 122-3
Austen, Edward, *see* Knight, Edward (previously Austen)
Austen, Francis, 118, 123, 126
Austen, George (Jane Austen's brother), 117-8
Austen, George (Jane Austen's father), 117, 118-9, 121, 122-3, 125
Austen, James, 117, 118, 121, 122
Austen, Jane:
  and the French Revolution, 120
  and the Prince Regent, 125-6
  author:

INDEX

of women, 8, 10-11, 13, 80-1,
90
prison, 148-9
works on, 9, 11, 80, 82-3
economics, 99-101, 102-103
religion, 102
science, 9, 91, 93-7, 101, 102,
104
Egerton, Thomas, publisher, 124–5
Electricity, 49-50, 97-8
Elgin marbles, 20
Elizabeth I, 62
Elizabeth, Princess, Landgravine
of Hesse-Homburg, 36, 37
Elopement, 42, 78
Emma, 125, 126
Enchmarch, Sarah, 12, 16, 17
Ennui, 85
Ernest, King of Hanover
(previously Duke of
Cumberland), 38
*Essay on the Noble Science of
Self-justification*, 81
European Magazine, 20-1, 22, 27
Exeter, 15-16, 69, 74, 76
Exmouth, 66, 72, 73, 74

Faraday, Michael, 9, 91, 97-8, 104
Fatal Marriage, The, play, 44
Firth, Colin, 129
Flamsteed, John, 33, 35
Fliedner, Theodor, 153
Fowle, Reverend Thomas, 120,
126
Fowles, John, 26
Franklin, Benjamin, 56
French Revolution, 10, 56-8, 59,
92, 120

Fry, Elizabeth (previously
Gurney):
anxiety and depression, 14,
145–7, 152, 154, 155
birth and early years, 144-5
character and appearance, 145–6,
148, 154
Christian faith, 10, 145-6, 154
death and legacy, 155
financial problems, 147, 151-2
ministry:
coastguard library project,
152-3
Institution for Nursing Sisters,
153-4
prison reform, 147-50
Quaker minister, 14, 146-7,
152
women being transported, 151
on position of women, 14
relationship with husband, 11-12,
146, 154
visited at Newgate by Maria
Edgeworth, 88, 154
Fry, Joseph:
financial problems, 147, 151-2
marriage, 11-12, 146, 154

Gambling, 85, 114, 148
Garrick, David, 43
Garson, Greer, 128
Geological Society, The, 14, 162,
164, 166
Geology, 157, 162, 166
George II, King, 28
George III, King:
illness and death, 7, 45
patronage of, 19, 21, 32, 45